SELECTED POEMS

OF

CATULLUS

CATULLUS

SELECTED POEMS

OF

CATULLUS

Translated by Carl Sesar

Line drawings by Arlene Dubanevich

Afterword by David Konstan

Mason & Lipscomb PUBLISHERS   NEW YORK

Copyright © 1974 by Carl Sesar

ISBN: 0-88405-085-8

Library of Congress Catalog Card Number: 73-92446

Printed in the United States of America

First Printing

Library of Congress Cataloging in Publication Data

Catullus, C. Valerius.
   Selected poems of Catullus.

   Latin and English on opposite pages.
   Bibliography: p.
   I. Sesar, Carl, 1933-   ed.   II. Title.
PA6274.A25   1974   874'.01   73-92446
ISBN: 0-88405-077-7
ISBN: 0-88405-085-8 (pbk.)

To Moe and Kate

TRANSLATOR'S NOTE

CATULLUS was born in the town of Verona, 250 miles north of Rome, in about 84 B.C. He lived and wrote in both Rome and Verona, stayed at times in Tibur, a suburb of Rome, and at Sirmio, a peninsula in present-day Lake Garda, and traveled as far as Bithynia and a few other places out in Asia Minor. He died at the age of 30 or so, in about 54 B.C.

Of his works, a total of 113 poems and a few fragments survive. Fragments aside, I translated all but 7 long poems and a scattered 7 others. The rest are arranged in their traditional order and numbering with a facing Latin text. They're all short, personal lyrics written in his own voice, and are the poems I felt most fully and love the best.

I want to thank the members of the Classics Department at Wesleyan University for their warm encouragement, especially my dear friend David Konstan, who was always ready with knowledge, understanding and good advice whenever I needed it.

Carl Sesar

Middletown, Connecticut
September 5, 1973

. . . at non effugies meos iambos.

. . . but you won't get away from my poems.

I

Cui dono lepidum nouum libellum
arido modo pumice expolitum?
Corneli, tibi: namque tu solebas
meas esse aliquid putare nugas;
iam tum cum ausus es unus Italorum
omne aeuum tribus explicare cartis
doctis, Iuppiter, et laboriosis:
quare habe tibi quidquid hoc libelli
qualecumque; quod, o patrona uirgo,
plus uno maneat perenne saeclo.

1

Who do I give this neat little book to
all new and polished up and ready to go?
You, Cornelius, because you always thought
there was something to this stuff of mine,
and were the one man in Italy with guts enough
to lay out all history in a couple of pages,
a learned job, by god, and it took work.
So here's the book, for whatever it's worth
I want you to have it. And please, goddess,
see that it lasts for more than a lifetime.

II

Passer, deliciae meae puellae,
quicum ludere, quem in sinu tenere,
cui primum digitum dare appetenti
et acris solet incitare morsus,
cum desiderio meo nitenti
carum nescio quid lubet iocari,
et solaciolum sui doloris,
credo ut tum grauis acquiescat ardor:
tecum ludere sicut ipsa possem
et tristis animi leuare curas!

2

Hello, sparrow, my girl's little pet,
she plays around with you, holds you,
gives you her fingertip to peck at,
teasing, poking to make you bite harder,
and glows, lovely, her eyes flashing,
thinking, I know, of other sweet games
and things to soothe the pain a little
once the heavy burning need dies down.
I wish I could play with you like that
and ease my mind of my own deep trouble.

III

Lugete, o Veneres Cupidinesque,
et quantum est hominum uenustiorum.
passer mortuus est meae puellae,
passer, deliciae meae puellae.
quem plus illa oculis suis amabat:
nam mellitus erat suamque norat
ipsam tam bene quam puella matrem,
nec sese a gremio illius mouebat,
sed circumsiliens modo huc modo illuc
ad solam dominam usque pipiabat.
qui nunc it per iter tenebricosum
illuc, unde negant redire quemquam.
at uobis male sit, malae tenebrae
Orci, quae omnia bella deuoratis:
tam bellum mihi passerem abstulistis.
o factum male! o miselle passer,
tua nunc opera meae puellae
flendo turgiduli rubent ocelli.

3

Weep, my dears, Venus, Cupids,
and all of you beautiful people.
My girl's sparrow is dead.
My girl's little pet sparrow.
She loved him more than anything,
he was her sweet, he knew his lady
as a girl knows her own mother,
never flew from her lap, just
hopped all around, here, there,
chirping to her and to her alone.
Now he wanders that dark road
down, from where nothing returns.
You no good hell hole down there!
You feed on every pretty thing,
and take such a pretty sparrow away!
And you, you sorry little sparrow,
see what you've done. Because of you
my girl's been crying her eyes out.

V

Viuamus, mea Lesbia, atque amemus,
rumoresque senum seueriorum
omnes unius aestimemus assis.
soles occidere et redire possunt:
nobis cum semel occidit breuis lux,
nox est perpetua una dormienda.
da mi basia mille, deinde centum,
dein mille altera, dein secunda centum,
deinde usque altera mille, deinde centum.
dein, cum milia multa fecerimus,
conturbabimus illa, ne sciamus,
aut ne quis malus inuidere possit,
cum tantum sciat esse basiorum.

5

Let's you and me live it up, my Lesbia,
and make some love, and let old cranks
go cheap talk their damn fool heads off.
Maybe suns can set and come back up again,
but once the brief light goes out on us
the night's one long sleep forever.
First give me a kiss, a thousand kisses,
then a hundred, and then a thousand more,
then another hundred, and another thousand,
and keep kissing and kissing me so many times
we get all mixed up and can't count anymore,
that way nobody can give us the evil eye
trying to figure how many kisses we've got.

VI

Flaui, delicias tuas Catullo,
ni sint illepidae atque inelegantes,
uelles dicere nec tacere posses.
uerum nescio quid febriculosi
scorti diligis: hoc pudet fateri.
nam te non uiduas iacere noctes
nequiquam tacitum, cubile clamat
sertis ac Syrio fragrans oliuo,
puluinusque peraeque et hic et ille
attritus, tremulique quassa lecti
argutatio inambulatioque.
nam nil stupra ualet, nihil tacere.
cur? non tam latera ecfututa pandas,
ni tu quid facias ineptiarum.
quare, quidquid habes boni malique,
dic nobis. uolo te ac tuos amores
ad caelum lepido uocare uersu.

6

The girl can't be much on looks or brains
Flavius, or you'd tell Catullus all about her,
in fact, you'd never shut up about it.
Sure looks like you found a hot little bitch
though, maybe you're ashamed to admit it,
but you aren't sleeping nights by yourself,
don't try to play dumb, the mattress says so
with flowers, reeks of sweet Syrian olive oil,
pillows are all over the place, bashed in flat,
and the whole bed creaks and wobbles so much
it practically walks and talks. Besides,
if you haven't been fucking yourself silly
then why's your ass dragging the way it is?
So whatever's going on, for better or worse,
tell me. I'll put all of that loving in a
sweet little poem, and make you both famous.

VII

Quaeris, quot mihi basiationes
tuae, Lesbia, sint satis superque?
quam magnus numerus Libyssae harenae
lasarpiciferis iacet Cyrenis
oraclum Iouis inter aestuosi
et Batti ueteris sacrum sepulcrum,
aut quam sidera multa, cum tacet nox,
furtiuos hominum uident amores:
tam te basia multa basiare
uesano satis et super Catullo est,
quae nec pernumerare curiosi
possint nec mala fascinare lingua.

7

Just how many kisses do I want, Lesbia,
before I finally get my fill of you?
Add up all of the sands across Africa
from the drug markets of Cyrenaica
to Jupiter sweating in his hot temple
on down to the tomb of old man Battus,
or all the stars in the dead of night
watching folks making love on the sly,
and that's how many kisses it'll take
before crazy Catullus stops kissing you,
more than all of the curious can count
or bad-mouth with their mumbo-jumbo.

VIII

Miser Catulle, desinas ineptire,
et quod uides perisse perditum ducas.
fulsere quondam candidi tibi soles,
cum uentitabas quo puella ducebat
amata nobis quantum amabitur nulla.
ibi illa multa tum iocosa fiebant,
quae tu uolebas nec puella nolebat.
fulsere uere candidi tibi soles.
nunc iam illa non uolt: tu quoque inpotens noli,
nec quae fugit sectare, nec miser uiue,
sed obstinata mente perfer, obdura.
uale, puella. iam Catullus obdurat,
nec te requiret nec rogabit inuitam.
at tu dolebis, cum rogaberis nulla.
scelesta, uae te, quae tibi manet uita?
quis nunc te adibit? cui uideberis bella?
quem nunc amabis? cuius esse diceris?
quem basiabis? cui labella mordebis?
at tu, Catulle, destinatus obdura.

8

You feel bad, Catullus, but quit acting stupid
and face facts. What's lost is lost.
You had yourself some sunny days for a while,
just going along wherever she led you,
no girl ever got the loving you gave her.
A lot of laughs and good times they were too,
anything you wanted she never said no,
yes, those were some sunny days all right.
But she doesn't want you now, so forget her.
Don't chase her around, making yourself miserable,
make your mind up it's over, and stick to it.
Goodbye my girl. You heard Catullus, he's had it.
He doesn't need you, he won't bother you anymore.
You'll feel sorry though when nobody wants you.
Too bad, bitch! What are you going to do now?
Who'll visit you? Who'll think you're beautiful?
Who will you love? Whose girl will they call you?
Who else will you kiss and bite on his lips?
But you, Catullus, remember: it's finished.

IX

Verani, omnibus e meis amicis
antistans mihi milibus trecentis,
uenistine domum ad tuos penates
fratresque unanimos anumque matrem?
uenisti. o mihi nuntii beati!
uisam te incolumem audiamque Hiberum
narrantem loca, facta, nationes,
ut mos est tuus, applicansque collum
iucundum os oculosque suauiabor.
o quantum est hominum beatiorum,
quid me laetius est beatiusue?

9

Veranius, my best friend, dearer to me than
any thousand friends I know, is it true
that you've come back home again, come home
to your loving brothers, your elderly mother?
It is true. And what beautiful news to me!
I'll see you safe and sound, listen to you
tell all about Hiberia, people, places, things
the way you always do, hug you by the neck,
kiss you on the mouth and those eyes I love . . .
So how do you do, all of you happy people!
Can anybody around be any happier than I am?

X

Varus me meus ad suos amores
uisum duxerat e foro otiosum,
scortillum, ut mihi tum repente uisum est,
non sane illepidum neque inuenustum.
huc ut uenimus, incidere nobis
sermones uarii, in quibus, quid esset
iam Bithynia, quo modo se haberet,
et quonam mihi profuisset aere.
respondi id quod erat, nihil neque ipsis
nec praetoribus esse nec cohorti,
cur quisquam caput unctius referret,
praesertim quibus esset irrumator
praetor, non faceret pili cohortem.
'at certe tamen,' inquiunt 'quod illic
natum dicitur esse, comparasti
ad lecticam homines.' Ego, ut puellae
unum me facerem beatiorem,
'non' inquam 'mihi tam fuit maligne,
ut, prouincia quod mala incidisset,
non possem octo homines parare rectos.'
at mi nullus erat neque hic neque illic,
fractum qui ueteris pedem grabati
in collo sibi collocare posset.
hic illa, ut decuit cinaediorem,
'quaeso' inquit 'mihi, mi Catulle, paulum
istos commoda: nam uolo ad Serapim
deferri.' 'mane' inquii puellae,
'istud quod modo dixeram me habere,
fugit me ratio: meus sodalis,

I'm hanging around the Forum when Varus
drags me off to meet this girl of his,
a cute little piece I see right away,
nothing dumb or sloppy about her—anyway,
we get to her place, and talking about one thing
or another they ask me what's what in Bithynia,
how was the action, did I make any money,
so I tell them just what it was,
that from the local yokels up, nobody,
the governor or us office boys,
made a goddamn thing, especially with
that cocksucker of a praetor who wouldn't
give you the hair off his . . . 'All right,' they say,
'but you must've made a deal on litter bearers,
you know, Buy Bithynian, We Breed the Best?'
So to be a big shot in front of the girl, I say,
'Look, it never got that tough for me, even if
I did land in some lousy province. In fact
I managed to pick up eight strong boys for myself.'
Now I don't have a boy here, there, or anywhere,
who could collar the busted leg off of an old sofa,
but what's her name (it figures with these little whores)
chimes in with, 'Oh please, Catullus dear,
be nice and lend them to me for a little while?
I wanna take a ride to Serapis.' 'Whoa,' I say.
'What I just said, well see, I forgot.
I mean my friend—Gaius Cinna?—they're his.
He uses them, or I, makes no difference,
he lets me use them just like they were mine . . .

Cinna est Gaius, is sibi parauit.
uerum, utrum illius an mei, quid ad me?
utor tam bene quam mihi pararim.
sed tu insulsa male et molesta uiuis,
per quam non licet esse neglegentem.'

but you're a regular pain in the ass, miss,
nobody can say anything with you around.'

XI

Furi et Aureli, comites Catulli,
siue in extremos penetrabit Indos,
litus ut longe resonante Eoa
tunditur unda,

siue in Hyrcanos Arabesque molles,
seu Sacas sagittiferosue Parthos,
siue quae septemgeminus colorat
aequora Nilus,

siue trans altas gradietur Alpes,
Caesaris uisens monimenta magni,
Gallicum Rhenum horribilesque ulti-
mosque Britannos,

omnia haec, quaecumque feret uoluntas
caelitum, temptare simul parati,
pauca nuntiate meae puellae
non bona dicta.

cum suis uiuat ualeatque moechis,
quos simul complexa tenet trecentos,
nullum amans uere, sed identidem omnium
ilia rumpens:

nec meum respectet, ut ante, amorem,
qui illius culpa cecidit uelut prati
ultimi flos, praetereunte postquam
tactus aratro est.

11

Furius, Aurelius, right with Catullus
if he'd go out past the limits of India
where the eastern ocean pounds upon the shore
with far sounding waves,

or to the soft lands, Arabia, Hyrcania,
through Sacia, Parthian bowman country,
into regions the seven-fingered Nile stains
dark with its waters,

or if he marched across the towering Alps
to look out over great Caesar's monuments
from the Gallic Rhine to the farthest removed
wild tribes of Britain,

companions ready to brave all this with me
and whatever else heaven's will has in store,
just deliver this brief message to my girl,
meant not to be kind.

Let her enjoy herself with her cheap lovers,
clamp them up between her legs by the hundreds,
say it's love, while one after another she
breaks them inside her,

but let her not look to my love anymore.
After all she's done, it fell, like a flower
at the edge of a field that the plow barely
touches in passing.

XII

Marrucine Asini, manu sinistra
non belle uteris in ioco atque uino,
tollis lintea neglegentiorum.
hoc salsum esse putas? fugit te, inepte:
quamuis sordida res et inuenusta est.
non credis mihi? crede Pollioni
fratri, qui tua furta uel talento
mutari uelit: est enim leporum
disertus puer ac facetiarum.
quare aut hendecasyllabos trecentos
exspecta, aut mihi linteum remitte,
quod me non mouet aestimatione,
uerum est mnemosynum mei sodalis.
nam sudaria Saetaba ex Hiberis
miserunt mihi muneri Fabullus
et Veranius: haec amem necesse est
ut Veraniolum meum et Fabullum.

12

It's not nice to use your left hand like that
at the table, Asinius, everybody busy laughing
and drinking, and you stealing their napkins.
You think it's funny? Guess again, creep,
it's as lowlife as you can get, not even cute.
Don't take my word for it, ask your brother
Pollio, a decent kid, with brains, who would
probably pay plenty to buy off all your thefts.
Now, you can either end up in more of my poems,
or give me my napkins and I'll forget about it.
Not that they're worth a whole lot either,
they happen to be souvenirs from some friends
of mine, Fabullus and Veranius, who sent them
to me all the way from Hiberia, and I love them,
Fabullus, Veranius, the napkins, and all.

XIII

Cenabis bene, mi Fabulle, apud me
paucis, si tibi di fauent, diebus,
si tecum attuleris bonam atque magnam
cenam, non sine candida puella
et uino et sale et omnibus cachinnis.
haec si, inquam, attuleris, uenuste noster,
cenabis bene: nam tui Catulli
plenus sacculus est aranearum.
sed contra accipies meros amores,
seu quid suauius elegantiusue est:
nam unguentum dabo, quod meae puellae
donarunt Veneres Cupidinesque,
quod tu cum olfacies, deos rogabis,
totum ut te faciant, Fabulle, nasum.

13

You're invited to a feast, Fabullus, my place,
it could be any day now, if you're lucky,
and if you bring a lot of good food with you,
better bring a girl along while you're at it,
and some wine, and all the latest jokes also.
As I say, you bring all this over, my friend,
and you're invited, because your Catullus
has a money bag full of spiders inside.
On the other hand, you get sweet love itself,
or what's sweeter, if anything, because I'm
providing a scent my girl always has on her,
the one she got straight from Venus and Cupid.
Get a whiff of that, Fabullus, and you'll be
praying the gods made you one big nose all over.

XIV

Ni te plus oculis meis amarem,
iucundissime Calue, munere isto
odissem te odio Vatiniano:
nam quid feci ego quidue sum locutus,
cur me tot male perderes poetis?
isti di mala multa dent clienti,
qui tantum tibi misit impiorum.
quod si, ut suspicor, hoc nouum ac repertum
munus dat tibi Sulla litterator,
non est me male, sed bene ac beate,
quod non dispereunt tui labores.
di magni, horribilem et sacrum libellum!
quem tu scilicet ad tuum Catullum
misti, continuo ut die periret,
Saturnalibus, optimo dierum!
non non hoc tibi, salse, sic abibit.
nam, si luxerit, ad librariorum
curram scrinia, Caesios, Aquinos,
Suffenum, omnia colligam uenena,
ac te his suppliciis remunerabor.
uos hinc interea ualete abite
illuc, unde malum pedem attulistis,
saecli incommoda, pessimi poetae.

14

Calvus old buddy, if I didn't love you
as much as I do, I'd hate you just as much
as Vatinius does. It's this gift you gave me.
What the hell did I do, what did I say,
that you annihilate me with all these poets?
And which damn client of yours was it who
sent you a collection of criminals like this?
Unless maybe it was Sulla, the big professor,
giving you a first edition or something,
then I don't mind, that's fine and dandy,
at least you're not his lawyer for nothing.
But god almighty, what a holy mess of a book!
And you right away send it off to your Catullus
just before the holidays, so that he can die
on the biggest Saturday night of the year!
Oh no, wise guy, you won't get away with it.
Come tomorrow morning I'm off to the bookstore,
I'll clean the shelves out of all the poisons,
all the Caesius, and Aquinus, and Suffenus,
wrap them up with my prayers, and pay you back.
In the meantime, you characters here, bye-bye,
back on the same crooked feet you limped in on,
times are bad enough without you lousy poets.

XIVa

Si qui forte mearum ineptiarum
lectores eritis manusque uestras
non horrebitis admouere nobis . . .

14a

Maybe some of you will read my stuff,
as clumsy as it is, and not even feel
dirty about putting your hands on me . . .

XV

Commendo tibi me ac meos amores,
Aureli. ueniam peto pudentem,
ut, si quicquam animo tuo cupisti,
quod castum expeteres et integellum,
conserues puerum mihi pudice,
non dico a populo: nihil ueremur
istos, qui in platea modo huc modo illuc
in re praetereunt sua occupati:
uerum a te metuo tuoque pene
infesto pueris bonis malisque.
quem tu qua lubet, ut lubet, moueto,
quantum uis, ubi erit foris paratum:
hunc unum excipio, ut puto, pudenter.
quod si te mala mens furorque uecors
in tantam inpulerit, sceleste, culpam,
ut nostrum insidiis caput lacessas,
a tum te miserum malique fati,
quem attractis pedibus patente porta
percurrent raphanique mugilesque.

15

I want you to take care of my boy friend,
Aurelius. All I ask is one simple favor,
that, if in your heart you ever desired
to preserve one thing clean and undefiled,
you'll keep the kid nice and pure for me.
I don't mean from others, I'm not afraid
of those folks out there in the streets
walking around minding their own business,
it's you, and your prick, the polluter
of good and bad boys both, that scares me.
Now you can go whip it out and use it
whenever you want, on anyone or anything,
except for this kid, that's all I ask.
But, if you're just plain stupid, or go
crazy enough to try it, you back-stabbing
son of a bitch, then I weep for you now,
ankles bound, bare-assed, gate wide open,
with catfish and carrots rammed up your hole.

XVI

Pedicabo ego uos et irrumabo,
Aureli pathice et cinaede Furi,
qui me ex uersiculis meis putastis,
quod sunt molliculi, parum pudicum.
nam castum esse decet pium poetam
ipsum, uersiculos nihil necesse est,
qui tum denique habent salem ac leporem,
si sunt molliculi ac parum pudici,
et quod pruriat incitare possint,
non dico pueris, sed his pilosis
qui duros nequeunt mouere lumbos.
uos, quod milia multa basiorum
legistis, male me marem putatis?
pedicabo ego uos et irrumabo.

16

Up your ass and in your mouth
Aurelius, you too Furius, you cocksuckers,
calling me dirt because my poems
have naughty naughty words in them.
Just the poet's got to be a boy scout
fellas, not his goddamn poems.
Anyway look, they've got wit, sass,
and sure they're lewd and lascivious,
and can get somebody pretty hard-up too,
I mean not just young kids, but you hairy guys
who can barely get your stiff asses going,
so just because you read about a lot of kisses
you want to put something nasty on me as a man?
Fuck you, up your ass and in your mouth.

XVII

O Colonia, quae cupis ponte ludere longo,
et salire paratum habes, sed uereris inepta
crura ponticuli axulis stantis in rediuiuis,
ne supinus eat cauaque in palude recumbat;
sic tibi bonus ex tua pons libidine fiat,
in quo uel Salisubsili sacra suscipiantur:
munus hoc mihi maximi da, Colonia, risus.
quendam municipem meum de tuo uolo ponte
ire praecipitem in lutum per caputque pedesque,
uerum totius ut lacus putidaeque paludis
liuidissima maximeque est profunda uorago.
insulsissimus est homo, nec sapit pueri instar
bimuli tremula patris dormientis in ulna.
cui cum sit uiridissimo nupta flore puella
et puella tenellulo delicatior haedo,
adseruanda nigerrimis diligentius uuis,
ludere hanc sinit ut lubet, nec pili facit uni,
nec se subleuat ex sua parte, sed uelut alnus
in fossa Liguri iacet suppernata securi,
tantundem omnia sentiens quam si nulla sit usquam.
talis iste meus stupor nil uidet, nihil audit,
ipse qui sit, utrum sit an non sit, id quoque nescit.
nunc eum uolo de tuo ponte mittere pronum,
si pote stolidum repente excitare ueternum;
et supinum animum in graui derelinquere caeno,
ferream ut soleam tenaci in uoragine mula.

Colonians, you folks here want a new long bridge,
you're all set for the festival, but the old wreck's
on its last legs and propped up so much already
it's liable to buckle and lay down in the mud anytime.
So here's how to get the good bridge you long for,
guaranteed to hold up under a Salisubsilian stomp:
do me a favor, my friends, and give me a good laugh.
I want a townsman of mine to go off your bridge
ass backwards and kicking right down in the muck,
and I mean way down, into the deepest and blackest
pit of slime out there in the whole stinking swamp.
The man's a dumbbell, he doesn't know any better
than a two-year-old rocking in his daddy's arms.
He married himself a girl, a regular flower in bloom,
a girl tender and delicious, a frisky little lamb
to be guarded real careful, like your juiciest grapes,
and he lets her run around loose, couldn't care less,
hell, he won't even go get some himself, he lays there
pole-axed and paralyzed like some log in a ditch,
knowing about as much as if he weren't there at all.
And that's my stupid, sees nothing, hears nothing,
doesn't know who he is, where he is, or if he is.
So I want to send him head first off the bridge,
maybe all of a sudden the stiff'll start moving
and leave his slow mind flat out behind him,
like a mule shakes a shoe that got stuck in the mud.

XXI

Aureli, pater esuritionum,
non harum modo, sed quot aut fuerunt
aut sunt aut aliis erunt in annis,
pedicare cupis meos amores.
nec clam: nam simul es, iocaris una,
haerens ad latus omnia experiris.
frustra: nam insidias mihi instruentem
tangam te prior irrumatione.
atque si faceres satur, tacerem:
nunc ipsum id doleo, quod esurire
mellitus puer et sitire discet.
quare desine, dum licet pudico,
ne finem facias, sed irrumatus.

21

Aurelius, you father of every hunger
there is, or was, or ever will be,
you want to make my boy friend now.
It's no secret: you're right there
with the funny jokes, getting in close,
feeling him up, you try everything.
Forget it. I'm wise to your tricks
and you can go suck my cock first.
I'd shut up if you ever got enough,
what bothers me now is a nice kid
might get hungry and thirsty like you,
so quit while you can, before you
end up eating a mouthful of me.

.

AURELIUS

XXII

Suffenus iste, Vare, quem probe nosti,
homo est uenustus et dicax et urbanus,
idemque longe plurimos facit uersus.
puto esse ego illi milia aut decem aut plura
perscripta, nec sic ut fit in palimpsesto
relata: cartae regiae, noui libri,
noui umbilici, lora rubra, membranae
derecta plumbo et pumice omnia aequata.
haec cum legas tu, bellus ille et urbanus
Suffenus unus caprimulgus aut fossor
rursus videtur: tantum abhorret ac mutat.
hoc quid putemus esse? qui modo scurra
aut si quid hac re scitius uidebatur,
idem infaceto est infacetior rure,
simul poemata attigit, neque idem umquam
aeque est beatus ac poema cum scribit:
tam gaudet in se tamque se ipse miratur.
nimirum idem omnes fallimur, neque est quisquam
quem non in aliqua re uidere Suffenum
possis. suus cuique attributus est error,
sed non uidemus manticae quod in tergo est.

Take Suffenus, now you know the guy, Varus,
handsome, good talker, knows his way around,
well he writes poetry also, in big shipments.
I think he's got thousands, maybe millions
copied out, I don't mean in rough draft either:
fancy imperial stock, new rolls, new pegs,
thongs of red leather, sheepskin slip covers,
lines ruled, edges trimmed, the whole works.
Then you read them. Suddenly your suave and
sophisticated Suffenus turns into a goat milker,
a shit shoveler from the mountains. It's grim!
What's going on anyway? Here he is, sharp,
looks like he could slice you down in a word,
but the minute he starts fooling with poetry,
watch out, he's clumsier than a hick is clumsy.
And he's never happier than when writing a poem,
or more pleased, he thinks he's just wonderful!
Okay, it's true, we all do it, there's nobody
who isn't a Suffenus in one thing or another.
Everybody has a pack of faults on his shoulders,
if heads were on backwards we'd all see our own.

XXIII

Furi, cui neque seruus est neque arca
nec cimex neque araneus neque ignis,
uerum est et pater et nouerca, quorum
dentes uel silicem comesse possunt:
est pulcre tibi cum tuo parente
et cum coniuge lignea parentis,
nec mirum: bene nam ualetis omnes,
pulcre concoquitis, nihil timetis,
non incendia, non graues ruinas,
non facta impia, non dolos ueneni,
non casus alios periculorum.
atqui corpora sicciora cornu
aut siquid magis aridum est habetis
sole et frigore et esuritione,
quare non tibi sit bene ac beate?
a te sudor abest, abest saliua,
mucusque et mala pituita nasi.
hanc ad munditiem adde mundiorem,
quod culus tibi purior salillo est,
nec toto decies cacas in anno,
atque id durius est faba et lapillis,
quod tu si manibus teras fricesque,
non umquam digitum inquinare posses.
haec tu commoda tam beata, Furi,
noli spernere nec putare parui,
et sestertia quae soles precari
centum desine: nam sat es beatus.

23

Maybe you don't have money or slaves, Furius,
or heat in the house, or a pot to piss in,
but you've got your dad, and a new mother too,
both with teeth that can split rock and eat it,
and it's beautiful the way you live together
with the old man and his stick of a wife,
and no wonder: you're all good and healthy,
have fine digestions, not a care in the world,
no fires, heavy damages, criminal thefts,
poisonous plots or any other possible hazards.
Besides, what with your body all dried out
and tougher than toenails, living in the
fresh air and sunshine on a starvation diet,
how in the hell can you help but be happy?
You're never bothered with sweat or saliva,
or phlegm, or snot running out of your nose,
and, to top off all of these good things yet,
your ass is as clean as a salt lick, seeing
you don't take a shit more than ten times a year,
and that's harder than a dry bean or pebble,
you can pick it up, rub it in your hands,
and you won't even get your fingers dirty!
With blessings of life such as this, Furius,
don't keep complaining about how poor you are,
and quit coming around asking for that loan
of a hundred—you're rich enough already.

XXIV

O qui flosculus es Iuuentiorum,
non horum modo, sed quot aut fuerunt
aut posthac aliis erunt in annis,
mallem diuitias Midae dedisses
isti, cui neque seruus est neque arca,
quam sic te sineres ab illo amari.
'qui? non est homo bellus?' inquies. est,
sed bello huic neque seruus est neque arca.
hoc tu quam lubet abice eleuaque:
nec seruum tamen ille habet neque arcam.

24

Beautiful young boys have been around
for a very long time, but you're the
little rosebud of them all, Juventius,
and I'd rather you gave him the gold
of King Midas before you let that man
with no money or slaves make love to you.
Isn't he a nice man, you ask? Oh yes,
but the nice man has no money or slaves.
Go ahead, toss it off if you want to,
he still hasn't got any money or slaves.

XXV

Cinaede Thalle, mollior cuniculi capillo
uel anseris medullula uel imula oricilla
uel pene languido senis situque araneoso,
idemque, Thalle, turbida rapacior procella,
cum diua mulier aries ostendit oscitantes,
remitte pallium mihi meum, quod inuolasti,
sudariumque Saetabum catagraphosque Thynos,
inepte, quae palam soles habere tamquam auita.
quae nunc tuis ab unguibus reglutina et remitte,
ne laneum latusculum manusque mollicellas
inusta turpiter tibi flagella conscribillent,
et insolenter aestues, uelut minuta magno
deprensa nauis in mari, uesaniente uento.

25

Look Thallus, you fat little fairy,
all flabby fluffy like a bunny's muff
or a goose's gash or a blob of earlobe
or an old limp prick bobbing in a web,
and then Thallus grabby as a whirlwind
when her lady divine sees nobody's looking,
better hand over my robe you lifted from me,
the imported towels and writing kit also,
you silly faggot, flashing them around
as if your daddy handed them down to you.
Get those sticky fingers off of them now,
before your furry buns and delicate paws
get streaked and sizzled by the nasty whip
and you start twitching your hot little box
like you never did before.

THALLUS

XXVI

Furi, uillula uestra non ad Austri
flatus opposita est neque ad Fauoni
nec saeui Boreae aut Apheliotae,
uerum ad milia quindecim et ducentos.
o uentum horribilem atque pestilentem!

26

Furius, your little place in the woods
isn't up against the winds of Auster or
Favonius or savage Boreas or Apheliotes,
but a note of fifteen grand two hundred,
an unhealthy draft to have on your back!

.

XXVII

Minister uetuli puer Falerni
inger mi calices amariores,
ut lex Postumiae iubet magistrae
ebrioso acino ebriosioris.
at uos quo lubet hinc abite, lymphae,
uini pernicies, et ad seueros
migrate. hic merus est Thyonianus.

27

Listen kid, go bring us something
decent to drink, you heard the lady,
she's smashed as a grape and wants
good old Falernian bubbly, the best.
Get out, water, you kill the wine,
move, go chase the squares instead,
over here we do only serious drinking.

XXVIII

Pisonis comites, cohors inanis,
aptis sarcinulis et expeditis,
Verani optime tuque mi Fabulle,
quid rerum geritis? satisne cum isto
uappa frigoraque et famem tulistis?
ecquidnam in tabulis patet lucelli
expensum, ut mihi, qui meum secutus
praetorem refero datum lucello?
'o Memmi, bene me ac diu supinum
tota ista trabe lentus irrumasti.'
sed, quantum uideo, pari fuistis
casu: nam nihilo minore uerpa
farti estis. pete nobiles amicos!
at uobis mala multa di deaeque
dent, opprobria Romuli Remique.

28

To Fabullus and Veranius, in care of
Piso & Associates, a two-bit outfit
traveling light, somewhere on the march:
Dear friends, how are things? Had enough
of hunger and cold with that half a prick?
Did you profit any from your losses yet
the way I did working for my praetor?
I put it down in the books as follows:
'Flat on my back all day today—Memmius
had me take it in the mouth this time.'
As far as I can see, you're no better off,
half a prick'll ram you hard as a whole one.
Run after big shots, that's what you get.
I say the hell with them all, they're a
goddamn disgrace to the good name of Rome.

XXIX

Quis hoc potest uidere, quis potest pati,
nisi impudicus et uorax et aleo,
Mamurram habere quod Comata Gallia
habebat ante et ultima Britannia?
cinaede Romule, haec uidebis et feres?
et ille nunc superbus et superfluens
perambulabit omnium cubilia,
ut albulus columbus aut Adoneus?
cinaede Romule, haec uidebis et feres?
es impudicus et uorax et aleo.
eone nomine, imperator unice,
fuisti in ultima occidentis insula,
ut ista uestra diffututa Mentula
ducenties comesset aut trecenties?
quid est alid sinistra liberalitas?
parum expatrauit an parum elluatus est?
paterna prima lancinata sunt bona,
secunda praeda Pontica, inde tertia
Hibera, quam scit amnis aurifer Tagus:
nunc Galliae timetur et Britanniae.
quid hunc, malum, fouetis? aut quid hic potest
nisi uncta deuorare patrimonia?
eone nomine urbis o piissimi
socer generque, perdidistis omnia?

29

Who but a greedy reckless gambler with lives
could stand by and let Mamurra get his hands
on what once belonged to people clear across
Gaul to the islands of Britain? Father of our
country, what pervert would put up with this?
And is he out now strutting around, arrogant,
still dripping from one bed into the other
like some overstuffed white peacock or Adonis?
What kind of pervert could put up with this?
You, a greedy, reckless gambler with lives.
And you too, our great commander-in-chief,
why was it you landed in the last islands west?
So that fucked-out Prickface friend of yours
could gobble his way through all those billions?
If this isn't misplaced generosity, what is?
Where's the limit to his ravenous appetite?
First he tore into his father's estate,
then the Pontican plunder, next the spoils
of Hiberia where even rivers run gold, and
now it's all Gaul and Britain to worry about.
Who needs him? What the hell is he good at
except for chomping up his big fat fortunes?
You mean for him you illustrious in-laws of
Rome's first family left the whole world in ruins?

XXX

Alfene immemor atque unanimis false sodalibus,
iam te nil miseret, dure, tui dulcis amiculi?
iam me prodere, iam non dubitas fallere, perfide?
num facta impia fallacum hominum caelicolis placent?
quae tu neglegis ac me miserum deseris in malis,
eheu quid faciant, dic, homines cuiue habeant fidem?
certe tute iubebas animam tradere, inique, me
inducens in amorem, quasi tuta omnia mi forent.
idem nunc retrahis te ac tua dicta omnia factaque
uentos irrita ferre ac nebulas aereas sinis.
si tu oblitus es, at di meminerunt, meminit Fides,
quae te ut paeniteat postmodo facti faciet tui.

30

You forget, Alfenus, you cheat on those who love you,
don't you even feel sorry for your sweet little friend?
Or how many more lies will you tell me, you bastard?
Think you please the gods making fools out of people?
But you don't care, you leave me feeling miserable,
and what's someone supposed to do, who can he believe?
It was you, you said to give myself up to you, liar,
leading me on into love, it all seemed so easy . . .
Now you walk out on me, and all you ever said or did
trails meaninglessly off into thin air and vanishes.
You may forget, but the gods remember, truth remembers,
and some day soon they'll make you pay for everything.

XXXI

Paene insularum, Sirmio, insularumque
ocelle, quascumque in liquentibus stagnis
marique uasto fert uterque Neptunus,
quam te libenter quamque laetus inuiso,
uix mi ipse credens Thyniam atque Bithynos
liquisse campos et uidere te in tuto.
o quid solutis est beatius curis,
cum mens onus reponit, ac peregrino
labore fessi uenimus larem ad nostrum,
desideratoque acquiescimus lecto?
hoc est quod unum est pro laboribus tantis.
salue, o uenusta Sirmio, atque ero gaude.
gaudete uosque, o Lydiae lacus undae,
ridete quidquid est domi cachinnorum.

31

Sirmio, you're about the prettiest little eyeful
of island in any lake or pool or big blue ocean
Neptune ever put anywhere—am I glad to see you!
I can't believe it. I'm back from the plains of
Bithynia, and here you are, as pretty as always!
Ah, this is the life, no more worries or cares,
I can take a load off my mind, relax, and after
all that hard traveling, come home and lay down
these weary bones in the bed that they long for.
This, this alone, makes it all worth the trouble.
So hello, lovely Sirmio, master's back, be happy!
And that goes for you too, Lydia's lake waters,
let's hear it, laugh, bring the whole house down!

XXXII

Amabo, mea dulcis Ipsithilla,
meae deliciae, mei lepores,
iube ad te ueniam meridiatum.
et si iusseris, illud adiuuato,
ne quis liminis obseret tabellam,
neu tibi lubeat foras abire,
sed domi maneas paresque nobis
nouem continuas fututiones.
uerum si quid ages, statim iubeto:
nam pransus iaceo et satur supinus
pertundo tunicamque palliumque.

32

Come on, my little Ipsithilla sweet,
you delicious piece, be a good girl
and let me take a nap with you.
Say the word, and if you do, be nice,
don't lock the door on me,
or pull a disappearing act,
but just stay home, warm it up,
and spread out nine straight fucks for me.
How about right now, in fact?
I mean I'm full, and flat on my back,
blasting through my underwear for you.

XXXIII

O furum optime balneariorum
Vibenni pater et cinaede fili,
nam dextra pater inquinatiore,
culo filius est uoraciore,
cur non exilium malasque in oras
itis? quandoquidem patris rapinae
notae sunt populo, et natis pilosas,
fili, nin potes asse uenditare.

There they are,
slickest of all the bath house chiselers,
father Vibennius and his slut of a son,
Daddy and his dirty deals
and Sonny with his hungry asshole.
Why don't you go take a trip someplace?
Everybody knows you're a cheap crook Dad,
and you couldn't peddle that hairy ass of yours
Sonnyboy, for a plugged nickel.

XXXV

Poetae tenero, meo sodali,
uelim Caecilo, papyre, dicas
Veronam ueniat, Noui relinquens
Comi moenia Lariumque litus.
nam quasdam uolo cogitationes
amici accipiat sui meique.
quare, si sapiet, uiam uorabit,
quamuis candida milies puella
euntem reuocet, manusque collo
ambas iniciens roget morari.
quae nunc, si mihi uera nuntiantur,
illum deperit impotente amore.
nam quo tempore legit incohatam
Dindymi dominam, ex eo misellae
ignes interiorem edunt medullam.
ignosco tibi, Sapphica puella
musa doctior, est enim uenuste
Magno Caecilio incohata Mater.

Page, I'd like you to tell Caecilius,
my poetic friend, to come to Verona,
to get out from behind those city walls
and far away from Larius for a while,
I have some advice I want him to hear
from a friend of his, and of mine also.
If he's smart, he'll run all the way,
no matter how many times his girl keeps
calling him, hugs him around the neck,
begging him to stay a little while longer.
Now she, if I heard the story right,
has fallen for him so bad it's hopeless—
she read his draft of *Lady of Dindymus*
and from then on the poor girl's been
on fire inside and out. Well, I don't
blame you, my wise little miss Sappho,
Caecilius is off to a beautiful start.

XXXVI

Annales Volusi, cacata carta,
uotum soluite pro mea puella,
nam sanctae Veneri Cupidinique
uouit, si sibi restitutus essem
desissemque truces uibrare iambos,
electissima pessimi poetae
scripta tardipedi deo daturam
infelicibus ustulanda lignis.
et hoc pessima se puella uidit
iocosis lepide uouere diuis.
nunc o caeruleo creata ponto,
quae sanctum Idalium Vriosque apertos
quaeque Ancona Cnidumque harundinosam
colis quaeque Amathunta quaeque Golgos
quaeque Durrachium Hadriae tabernam,
acceptum face redditumque uotum,
si non illepidum neque inuenustum est.
at uos interea uenite in ignem,
pleni ruris et infacetiarum
annales Volusi, cacata carta.

36

Annals of Volusius, you pile of shit,
come here, keep my girl friend honest.
See, she swore to holy Venus and Cupid
that if I just came back to her again
and quit flinging my nasty poems around,
she'd select the choicest works of the
lousiest poet and roast them over the
unholiest fire old slow foot can kindle.
Now it takes a bad girl to know what's
lousy, so, if the gods can take a joke,
here goes: 'O divine creation of the deep,
heavenly goddess of Idalium and wide-open
Urii, of Ancona and Cnidus, city of reeds,
sacred lady of Amathus and Golgi, and also
Dyrrachium, where the debris meets the sea,
please mark her vow as duly paid in full
with style and grace and no offense meant.'
Okay, let's go, into the fire with you,
come on, stupid, the whole sloppy mess,
Annals of Volusius, you pile of shit!

Salax taberna uosque contubernales,
a pilleatis nona fratribus pila,
solis putatis esse mentulas uobis,
solis licere, quidquid est puellarum,
confutuere et putare ceteros hircos?
an, continenter quod sedetis insulsi
centum an ducenti, non putatis ausurum
me una ducentos irrumare sessores?
atqui putate: namque totius uobis
frontem tabernae sopionibus scribam.
puella nam mi, quae mea sinu fugit,
amata tantum quantum amabitur nulla,
pro qua mihi sunt magna bella pugnata,
consedit istic. hanc boni beatique
omnes amatis, et quidem, quod indignum est,
omnes pusilli et semitarii moechi;
tu praeter omnes une de capillatis,
cuniculosae Celtiberiae fili,
Egnati, opaca quem bonum facit barba
et dens Hibera defricatus urina.

Whorehouse, and all you backroom soldier boys,
nine pillars down from the Brothers of the Beanie,
you think you're the only ones who've got the Tool?
Do the girls hand you special screwing permits?
You call the rest of us a herd of goats?
Well listen, I'll hand the whole crew of you,
200 at a time, sitting in a row with your feet
in your mouth, something better to suck on—
I'll plaster pricks all over the walls!
Because this girl of mine, who ran out on me,
(no girl will ever get the loving I gave her)
a girl who got me into one fight after another,
ends up inside, and all you high society glamor boys
sleep with her, which is a dirty shame, because
you're a pack of crawling, back-alley sneak fuckers.
But the worst of the lot, of all you curly headed wonders,
is that Celtiberian refugee from the rabbit country,
Egnatius. He's a black bearded phony, and on top of this,
he brushes his teeth with Spanish piss.

XXXVIII

Malest, Cornifici, tuo Catullo,
malest, me hercule, et laboriose,
et magis magis in dies et horas.
quem tu, quod minimum facillimumque est,
qua solatus es allocutione?
irascor tibi. sic meos amores?
paulum quid lubet allocutionis,
maestius lacrimis Simonideis.

38

It's all gone bad for me, Cornificius,
bad I'm telling you, it's wearing me down,
worse and worse, every hour, every day.
And you, when it'd be so easy, have you
said one kind word to make me feel better?
I'm angry. You call yourself a friend?
Say something, anything, sing a sad song,
make me cry the way the old Greeks could.

XXXIX

Egnatius, quod candidos habet dentes,
renidet usquequaque. si ad rei uentum est
subsellium, cum orator excitat fletum,
renidet ille: si ad pii rogum fili
lugetur, orba cum flet unicum mater,
renidet ille: quidquid est, ubicumque est,
quodcumque agit, renidet: hunc habet morbum,
neque elegantem, ut arbitror, neque urbanum.
quare monendum est te mihi, bone Egnati.
si urbanus esses aut Sabinus aut Tiburs,
aut parcus Vmber aut obesus Etruscus,
aut Lanuuinus ater atque dentatus,
aut Transpadanus, ut meos quoque attingam,
aut qui lubet, qui puriter lauit dentes,
tamen renidere usquequaque te nollem:
nam risu inepto res ineptior nulla est.
nunc Celtiber es: Celtiberia in terra,
quod quisque minxit, hoc sibi solet mane
dentem atque russam defricare gingiuam,
ut quo iste uester expolitior dens est,
hoc te amplius bibisse praedicet loti.

39

Egnatius has white teeth, that's why
he's always smiling. Go to court
when the lawyer's got the crowd in tears,
he smiles. At a family funeral,
a mother weeping at the grave of her only son,
he smiles. Whatever or wherever it is,
you name it, he smiles. It's sick
if you ask me, not nice or even civilized.
So let me tell you something Egnatius my man.
You could be Roman or Sabine or Tiburtine,
an Umbrian skinflint or a fat assed Etruscan,
or some bucktoothed black from Lanuvium,
or a Transpadane, just to mention my own,
anyone who cleans his teeth with fresh water,
and I still couldn't take your smiling all the time—
I mean there's nothing dumber than a dumb smile.
But now you're Celtiberian. In Celtiberian country
they take a leak and save it for the morning
to brush their teeth and rub their gums up red,
so the whiter and brighter your teeth sparkle,
the more piss of yours we know you've been drinking.

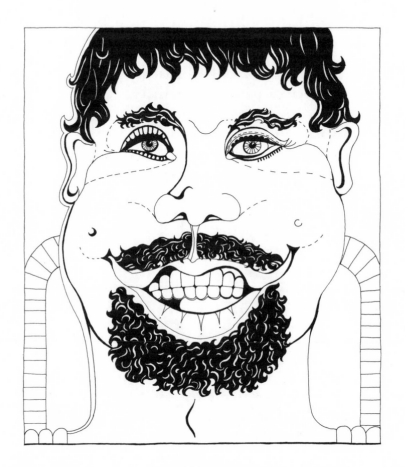

EGNATIUS

XL

Quaenam te mala mens, miselle Rauide,
agit praecipitem in meos iambos?
quis deus tibi non bene aduocatus
uecordem parat excitare rixam?
an ut peruenias in ora uulgi?
quid uis? qualubet esse notus optas?
eris, quandoquidem meos amores
cum longa uoluisti amare poena.

40

Lost your mind Ravidus, you poor ass,
landing smack into one of my poems like this?
Is some god getting you into trouble
because you didn't say your prayers right?
Or are you just out to get talked about?
What do you want? To be famous, never mind how?
Okay you will, and being that it's my girl you're after,
you're going to suffer for a long, long time.

XLI

Ameana puella defututa
tota milia me decem poposcit,
ista turpiculo puella naso,
decoctoris amica Formiani.
propinqui, quibus est puella curae,
amicos medicosque conuocate:
non est sana puella, nec rogare
qualis sit solet aes imaginosum.

41

Ameana, that fucked-out little bitch,
said she'd charge me ten thousand flat,
yeah, the one with the pushed in nose
who screws for that loser from Formiae.
Get together, you guardians of the kid,
call some friends or doctors or something—
the girl's out of her mind, and better
look in the mirror once in a while.

XLII

Adeste, hendecasyllabi, quot estis
omnes undique, quotquot estis omnes.
iocum me putat esse moecha turpis,
et negat mihi uestra reddituram
pugillaria, si pati potestis.
persequamur eam at reflagitemus.
quae sit, quaeritis? illa, quam uidetis
turpe incedere, mimice ac moleste
ridentem catuli ore Gallicani.
circumsistite eam, et reflagitate,
'moecha putida, redde codicillos,
redde, putida moecha, codicillos!'
non assis facis? o lutum, lupanar,
aut si perditius potes quid esse.
sed non est tamen hoc satis putandum.
quod si non aliud potest, ruborem
ferreo canis exprimamus ore.
conclamate iterum altiore uoce,
'moecha putida, redde codicillos,
redde, putida moecha, codicillos!'
sed nil proficimus, nihil mouetur.
mutanda est ratio modusque uobis,
siquid proficere amplius potestis:
'pudica et proba, redde codicillos.'

42

Calling all syllables! Calling all syllables!
Let's go! I need all the help I can get!
Some filthy whore's playing games with me
and won't give me back my manuscripts with
your pals inside! Are you going to let her?
Who is she, you ask? Well go take a look,
she's over there shaking her ass all around
and flashing smiles like a Pomeranian bitch.
Ready? Okay, line up and let her have it!
'O foul adulteress, O lascivious witch,
give me back my notebooks, you dirty bitch!'
What? Up yours, you say? You slut, tramp,
you've sunk so low you look up to see down!
Still, we can't let her get away like this,
if all else fails, at least let's see whether
we can force a blush from the hard-faced beast.
Try again, fellas, good and loud this time!
'O FOUL ADULTERESS, O LASCIVIOUS WITCH,
GIVE ME BACK MY NOTEBOOKS, YOU DIRTY BITCH!'
No use. It won't work. Nothing moves her.
We've got to switch to different tactics,
almost anything will work better than this.
'O maiden so modest, O virgin so pure . . .'

XLIII

Salue, nec minimo puella naso
nec bello pede nec nigris ocellis
nec longis digitis nec ore sicco
nec sane nimis elegante lingua,
decoctoris amica Formiani.
ten prouincia narrat esse bellam?
tecum Lesbia nostra comparatur?
o saeclum insapiens et infacetum!

43

Hello, you not so little-nosed
or cute-footed or dark-eyed
or long-fingered or dry-mouthed
or even very nice-tongued bitch
who screws for that loser from Formiae.
You're what they call beautiful?
They compare you to Lesbia?
How dumb can they get nowadays?

XLIV

O funde noster, seu Sabine seu Tiburs,
nam te esse Tiburtem autumant, quibus non est
cordi Catullum laedere, at quibus cordi est,
quouis Sabinum pignore esse contendunt,
sed seu Sabine siue uerius Tiburs,
fui libenter in tua suburbana
uilla, malamque pectore expuli tussim,
non inmerenti quam mihi meus uenter,
dum sumptuosas appeto, dedit, cenas.
nam, Sestianus dum uolo esse conuiua,
orationem in Antium petitorem
plenam ueneni et pestilentiae legi.
hic me grauedo frigida et frequens tussis
quassauit usque, dum in tuum sinum fugi,
et me recuraui otioque et urtica.
quare refectus maximas tibi grates
ago, meum quod non es ulta peccatum.
nec deprecor iam, si nefaria scripta
Sesti recepso, quin grauedinem et tussim
non mi, sed ipsi Sestio ferat frigus,
qui tunc uocat me, cum malum librum legi.

Old farm, maybe you're Sabine, maybe Tiburtine
(they say you're Tiburtine, well, at least folks
who don't like to get at Catullus, but others
will bet their bottom dollar that you're Sabine),
anyway, whatever you are, and that's Tiburtine,
was I glad to get up to your place and out of
the city, that cough in my chest was killing me—
not that I didn't ask for it, stuffing my greedy
belly full at every fancy dinner party in town.
I was all set for a big feast at Sestius' place,
so I read a speech of his, down with Antius, etc.,
a heaping mess dripping with poisons and plague,
it made me sick—I broke out into a cold sweat,
coughing and puking until I ran back to you and
took the cure: strict diet, thorn broth in bed.
It worked, and now that I'm better, thanks a lot
for not making me suffer, I paid for my mistake,
and I swear, if ever I go near that filthy crap
of Sestius again, bring on the coughs and puking,
but not to me, let him go choke his own guts out,
asking me to read that garbage when I'm eating.

XLVI

Iam uer egelidos refert tepores,
iam caeli furor aequinoctialis
iucundis Zephyri silescit aureis.
linquantur Phrygii, Catulle, campi
Nicaeaeque ager uber aestuosae:
ad claras Asiae uolemus urbes.
iam mens praetrepidans auet uagari,
iam laeti studio pedes uigescunt.
o dulces comitum ualete coetus,
longe quos simul a domo profectos
diuersae uarie uiae reportant.

46

And suddenly it's spring, warm and cool again,
here they come at last, soft whispering winds
to hush the mad raging of the equinoctial sky.
Time to go, Catullus, to leave the flat plains
of Phrygia, the rich farmlands of hot Nicaea—
we're off, to the glittering capitals of Asia!
My mind's in a whirl, can't wait to get going,
my feet are so happy they're moving without me . . .
Goodbye, my sweet friends and fellow travelers!
We set forth together, and now, far from home,
we scatter by different paths back to Rome again.

XLVII

Porci et Socration, duae sinistrae
Pisonis, scabies famesque mundi,
uos Veraniolo meo et Fabullo
uerpus praeposuit Priapus ille?
uos conuiuia lauta sumptuose
de die facitis, mei sodales
quaerunt in triuio uocationes?

47

Porcius and Socration, the two left hands
of Piso, the plague and crud of the earth,
does old half-a-prick prefer the two of you
to my good friends Fabullus and Veranius?
You mean he throws you big fancy parties
and banquets for brunch, while my crowd
goes prowling the streets for invitations?

XLVIII

Mellitos oculos tuos, Iuuenti,
siquis me sinat usque basiare,
usque ad milia basiem trecenta,
nec mi umquam uidear satur futurus,
non si densior aridis aristis
sit nostrae seges osculationis.

48

Just let me kiss those honeyed eyes,
Juventius, and if I could keep on
kissing until I was satisfied, I'd
never stop, not if a whole cornfield
of kisses grew thick all around us.

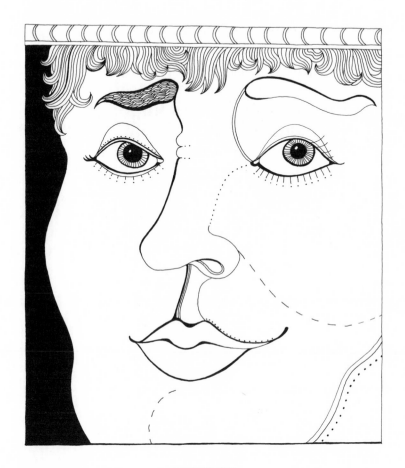

JUVENTIUS

XLIX

Disertissime Romuli nepotum,
quot sunt quotque fuere, Marce Tulli,
quotque post aliis erunt in annis,
gratias tibi maximas Catullus
agit pessimus omnium poeta,
tanto pessimus omnium poeta,
quanto tu optimus omnium patronus.

49

Most eloquent of the Sons of Romulus
there are, or were, or shall ever be
for ages to come, Marcus Tullius Cicero,
thanking you, I remain, yours truly,
Catullus, the lousiest poet of them all,
about the lousiest poet of them all
as much as you're the best of lawyers.

L

Hesterno, Licini, die otiosi
multum lusimus in meis tabellis,
ut conuenerat esse delicatos.
scribens uersiculos uterque nostrum
ludebat numero modo hoc modo illoc,
reddens mutua per iocum atque uinum.
atque illinc abii tuo lepore
incensus, Licini, facetiisque,
ut nec me miserum cibus iuuaret
nec somnus tegeret quiete ocellos,
sed toto indomitus furore lecto
uersarer, cupiens uidere lucem,
ut tecum loquerer simulque ut essem.
at defessa labore membra postquam
semimortua lectulo iacebant,
hoc, iucunde, tibi poema feci,
ex quo perspiceres meum dolorem.
nunc audax caue sis, precesque nostras,
oramus, caue despuas, ocelle,
ne poenas Nemesis reposcat a te.
est uemens dea: laedere hanc caueto.

50

It was quite a day yesterday, Licinius,
you came over, I broke out my writing kit,
and we had us such a wild time together
tossing off all those raw little verses,
one for you, one for me, laughing away,
drinking, that by the time it was over
and you went home, what with your charm
and wit, Licinius, I was on fire for you.
I felt so bad I couldn't eat anything,
couldn't sleep, I just lay there in bed
going crazy waiting for the sun to come up
so I could talk to you, be with you again.
But I'm so worn out now I can hardly move,
so, practically half-dead from my bedside,
here, beautiful, I wrote this poem for you.
Well, now you know what my trouble is.
And I'm warning you, don't get too smart,
and you'd better not turn me down either,
sweetheart, or Nemesis will take care of you.
She's a strict goddess, don't play with her.

LI

Ille mi par esse deo uidetur,
ille, si fas est, superare diuos,
qui sedens aduersus identidem te
spectat et audit

dulce ridentem, misero quod omnis
eripit sensus mihi: nam simul te,
Lesbia, aspexi, nihil est super mi
. . .

lingua sed torpet, tenuis sub artus
flamma demanat, sonitu suopte
tintinant aures, gemina teguntur
lumina nocte.

otium, Catulle, tibi molestum est:
otio exsultas nimiumque gestis:
otium et reges prius et beatas
perdidit urbes.

51

To me, that man seems to be one of the gods,
or to tell the truth, even more than a god,
sitting there face to face with you, forever
looking, listening

to you laughing sweetly, while poor me, I take
one look at you and I'm all torn up inside,
Lesbia, there's nothing left of me, I can't
make a sound, my tongue's

stuck solid, hot little fire flashes go
flickering through my body, my ears begin
ringing around in my head, my eyes black out,
shrouded in darkness . . .

This soft life is no good for you, Catullus,
you wallow in it, you don't know when to stop.
A soft life's already been the ruin of both
great kings and cities.

LII

Quid est, Catulle? quid moraris emori?
sella in curuli struma Nonius sedet,
per consulatum perierat Vatinius:
quid est, Catulle? quid moraris emori?

52

Why wait, Catullus? Go drop dead right now.
That cancer, Nonius, sits on a justice's seat
and Vatinius'll soon do his lying as president.
So why wait, Catullus? Drop dead right now.

LIII

Risi nescio quem modo e corona,
qui, cum mirifice Vatiniana
meus crimina Caluos explicasset,
admirans ait haec manusque tollens,
'di magni, salaputium disertum!'

53

I had to laugh. Some guy in the crowd,
after Calvus finished a terrific speech
exposing all the wicked deeds of Vatinius,
raised his hands in loving wonder, 'Man,'
he says, 'that little fuck sure can talk!'

LIVa

Irascere iterum meis iambis
inmerentibus, unice imperator.

54a

There you go getting mad at my poems again,
my innocent poems, you big, bad general, you.

LV

Oramus, si forte non molestum est,
demonstres ubi sint tuae tenebrae.
te Campo quaesiuimus minore,
te in Circo, te in omnibus libellis,
te in templo summi Iouis sacrato.
in Magni simul ambulatione
femellas omnes, amice, prendi,
quas uultu uidi tamen serenas.
a uelte, sic ipse flagitabam,
'Camerium mihi pessimae puellae.'
quaedam inquit, nudum reduc . . .
'en hic in roseis latet papillis.'
sed te iam ferre Herculei labos est.
tanto te in fastu negas, amice?
dic nobis ubi sis futurus, ede
audacter, committe, crede luci.
nunc te lacteolae tenent puellae?
si linguam clauso tenes in ore,
fructus proicies amoris omnes.
uerbosa gaudet Venus loquella.
uel, si uis, licet obseres palatum,
dum uestri sim particeps amoris.

55

Please, Camerius, I'm asking you nicely,
you mind telling me where you've been hiding?
I've been asking around in the park for you,
over at the Circus, in all the libraries,
even up on the hill at the temple of Jove.
Finally, my friend, I went to the Promenade,
walked right up to all the ladies and said,
'You bad, bad girls, give me my Camerius!'
They looked me right back straight in the eye,
and one of them opens her dress up in front,
'Here he is, in between my big, rosy tits!'
Boy, finding you is a job for Hercules already.
Maybe you're too good for us, is that it, pal?
Come on, talk, where the hell are you anyway,
let's get the whole story out in the open,
is it true the milk-white lovelies have got you?
If you don't give your tongue some exercise
you're going to waste a whole lot of loving,
you know how Venus likes to get talked about.
All right, go ahead, keep your mouth shut,
but leave just a little love left over for me.

LVI

O rem ridiculam, Cato, et iocosam,
dignamque auribus et tuo cachinno.
ride, quidquid amas, Cato, Catullum:
res est ridicula et nimis iocosa.
deprendi modo pupulum puellae
trusantem: hunc ego, si placet Dionae,
pro telo rigida mea cecidi.

56

Here's a good one for you Cato:
I caught a kid humping his lass,
and the chance was too good to pass,
a true son of Venus,
I whipped out my penis,
and pronged a piece off of his ass.

LVII

Pulcre conuenit improbis cinaedis,
Mamurrae pathicoque Caesarique.
nec mirum: maculae pares utrisque,
urbana altera et illa Formiana,
impressae resident nec eluentur:
morbosi pariter, gemelli utrique,
uno in lecticulo erudituli ambo,
non hic quam ille magis uorax adulter,
riuales socii puellularum.
pulcre conuenit improbis cinaedis.

57

They're beautiful together, the odd couple,
Mamurra, and Caesar his queen.
Naturally. You get two splats of shit together,
one from the city, the other from Formiae,
and you can never wash them off.
One's as sick as the other, twin diseases
in their little bed, with their little minds,
and both still fuck-hungry besides,
beating each other out after little girls.
They're beautiful together, the odd couple.

MAMURRA and CAESAR

LVIII

Caeli, Lesbia nostra, Lesbia illa,
illa Lesbia, quam Catullus unam
plus quam se atque suos amauit omnes,
nunc in quadriuiis et angiportis
glubit magnanimi Remi nepotes.

58

Caelius, our Lesbia, that Lesbia,
the Lesbia Catullus once loved
more than himself and all he owns,
now works streets and back alleys
groping big-hearted sons of Remus.

LIX

Bononiensis Rufa Rufulum fellat,
uxor Meneni, saepe quam in sepulcretis
uidistis ipso rapere de rogo cenam,
cum deuolutum ex igne prosequens panem
ab semiraso tunderetur ustore.

59

Rufa sucks her kid brother off, that's Menenius' wife,
you see her a lot stealing lunch in the graveyard
when she grabs a hunk of bread off the funeral fire
and the slob burning bodies has to beat her ass in.

LX

Num te leaena montibus Libystinis
aut Scylla latrans infima inguinum parte
tam mente dura procreauit ac taetra,
ut supplicis uocem in nouissimo casu
contemptam haberes, a nimis fero corde?

60

Were you dropped from an African she-cat
or the belly of a howling two-headed bitch
to get to be such a cold-blooded monster
you can turn your back on a man's last cry
as if he weren't there—are you human?

LXV

Etsi me assiduo confectum cura dolore
seuocat a doctis, Hortale, uirginibus,
nec potis est dulcis Musarum expromere fetus
mens animi, tantis fluctuat ipsa malis,
namque mei nuper Lethaeo gurgite fratris
pallidulum manans alluit unda pedem,
Troia Rhoeteo quem subter litore tellus
ereptum nostris obterit ex oculis . . .
alloquar, audiero numquam tua facta loquentem,
numquam ego te, uita frater amabilior,
aspiciam posthac. at certe semper amabo,
semper maesta tua carmina morte canam,
qualia sub densis ramorum concinit umbris
Daulias, absumpti fata gemens Ityli.
sed tamen in tantis maeroribus, Hortale, mitto
haec expressa tibi carmina Battiadae,
ne tua dicta uagis nequiquam credita uentis
effluxisse meo forte putes animo,
ut missum sponsi furtiuo munere malum
procurrit casto uirginis e gremio,
quod miserae oblitae molli sub ueste locatum,
dum aduentu matris prosilit, excutitur,
atque illud prono praeceps agitur decursu,
huic manat tristi conscius ore rubor.

Though I'm worn out with constant pain and sorrow,
and no fit company, Hortalus, for the learned maids
when my mind, unable to bring forth sweet children
by the Muses, tosses and turns in its own troubles,
for now the creeping tides of Lethe wash the death-
pale foot of my brother in their fathomless waters,
and he lies trampled under the earth, taken from
our sight, lost beneath the heavy coasts of Troy . . .
never will I speak to you, hear you talk of things,
never, O my brother, dearer to me than life, never
will I see you again. But I will love you always,
and always sing songs of mourning for your death,
just as deep within the shadows of the forest the
Daulian bird cries in sorrow for the fate of Itylus . . .
Still, for all of my grief, Hortalus, I send you
these translations of some verse by Callimachus,
so you won't think that what you said to me just
slipped from the vague wandering fog in my mind
the way an apple her boy friend sent her in secret
pops right out of a girl's innocent young breast
because, the poor thing, she forgot all about it
under her dress and jumped up when mother came in,
there it goes bouncing across the floor, her face
is red, she's so ashamed of herself she could cry.

LXVIII

Quod mihi fortuna casuque oppressus acerbo
conscriptum hoc lacrimis mittis epistolium,
naufragum ut eiectum spumantibus aequoris undis
subleuem et a mortis limine restituam,
quem neque sancta Venus molli requiescere somno
desertum in lecto caelibe perpetitur,
nec ueterum dulci scriptorum carmine Musae
oblectant, cum mens anxia peruigilat,
id gratum est mihi, me quoniam tibi dicis amicum,
muneraque et Musarum hinc petis et Veneris.
sed tibi ne mea sint ignota incommoda, Malli,
neu me odisse putes hospitis officium,
accipe, quis merser fortunae fluctibus ipse,
ne amplius a misero dona beata petas.
tempore quo primum uestis mihi tradita pura est,
iucundum cum aetas florida uer ageret,
multa satis lusi: non est dea nescia nostri,
quae dulcem curis miscet amaritiem.
sed totum hoc studium luctu fraterna mihi mors
abstulit. o misero frater adempte mihi,
tu mea tu moriens fregisti commoda, frater,
tecum una tota est nostra sepulta domus,
omnia tecum una perierunt gaudia nostra,
quae tuus in uita dulcis alebat amor.
cuius ego interitu tota de mente fugaui
haec studia atque omnes delicias animi.
quare, quod scribis, 'Veronae turpe, Catulle,
esse, quod hic quisquis de meliore nota
frigida deserto tepefactat membra cubili,'

That after such a bitter run of luck you should
send this letter to me, written with your tears,
in hope I might save a man wrecked and tossed by
foaming seas and take him from the door of death,
one whom neither holy Venus allows gentle sleep
as he lies deserted in his lonely bed, unloved,
nor the Muses console with sweet songs of ancient
poets, when his mind suffers through the night,
for this I thank you, because you call me friend,
and turn to me for the gifts of poetry and love.
But so you may not be unaware of my own troubles,
Mallius, or think I avoid my duties to a friend,
listen to one sunk himself in the seas of fortune
and do not ask for more blessings than I can give.
From the time I first put on a man's white robes,
as a youth in full flower, seeking his pleasure,
I played the game often enough. The goddess who
mixes sweet cares with bitter is no stranger to me.
But I've had no heart at all for this ever since
my brother's death—O my brother, taken from me,
you are dead, and with you all I have, my brother,
all is shattered, lost, all my house is buried,
my every happiness perished to the last with you,
everything that in life your sweet love nourished!
Now, with his death, my thoughts have turned from
all those pursuits in which I once took pleasure,
so that when you write, 'It's a shame, Catullus,
you in Verona, while every young playboy in town
keeps himself warm in the bed you called your own,'

id, Malli, non est turpe, magis miserum est.
ignosces igitur si, quae mihi luctus ademit,
haec tibi non tribuo munera, cum nequeo.
nam, quod scriptorum non magna est copia apud me,
hoc fit, quod Romae uiuimus: illa domus,
illa mihi sedes, illic mea carpitur aetas,
huc una ex multis capsula me sequitur.
quod cum ita sit, nolim statuas nos mente maligna
id facere aut animo non satis ingenuo,
quod tibi non utriusque petenti copia posta est:
ultro ego deferrem, copia siqua foret.

this is no shame, Mallius, it's a plain sad fact.
Forgive me, then, if I don't send you those gifts
that grief has already taken away from me. I can't.
I don't keep much of a supply of books here either,
since, of course, I live in Rome. That's my home,
my house is there, that's where my life is spent,
and here I take only one small case along with me.
Well, this is how it is, and I wouldn't want you
to think it's out of spite or any lack of sympathy
that you haven't received all you've asked me for,
I'd send it to you unasked if I had what to give.

LXIX

Noli admirari, quare tibi femina nulla,
Rufe, uelit tenerum supposuisse femur,
non si illam rarae labefactes munere uestis
aut perluciduli deliciis lapidis.
laedit te quaedam mala fabula, qua tibi fertur
ualle sub alarum trux habitare caper.
hunc metuunt omnes, neque mirum: nam mala ualde est
bestia, nec quicum bella puella cubet.
quare aut crudelem nasorum interfice pestem,
aut admirari desine cur fugiunt.

69

You can stop wondering why no woman around
is willing to spread her legs for you, Rufus,
not even if you buy her expensive dresses
or fancy diamond sparklers to soften her up.
The trouble is, word's out on you that says
there's a wild goat living under your armpits.
They're all scared of it, naturally. I mean
that's no animal for a nice girl to sleep with.
So wipe out that deadly nose-killer of yours
or just quit wondering why they all run away.

LXX

Nulli se dicit mulier mea nubere malle
quam mihi, non si se Iuppiter ipse petat.
dicit: sed mulier cupido quod dicit amanti,
in uento et rapida scribere oportet aqua.

70

My woman says there's nobody she'd rather marry
than me, not even Jupiter himself if he asked her.
She says, but what a woman says to a hungry lover
you might as well scribble in wind and swift water.

LXXI

Si cui iure bono sacer alarum obstitit hircus,
aut si quem merito tarda podagra secat,
aemulus iste tuus, qui uestrum exercet amorem,
mirifice est a te nactus utrumque malum.
nam quotiens futuit, totiens ulciscitur ambos:
illam affligit odore, ipse perit podagra.

71

If anybody had a good dose of stink coming,
or caught the rot and got what he asked for,
the guy taking turns with your girl friend is
a regular whiz, he got them both from you.
Now whenever they fuck they suffer together,
she passes out from the odor, he with the pain.

LXXII

Dicebas quondam solum te nosse Catullum,
Lesbia, nec prae me uelle tenere Iouem.
dilexi tum te non tantum ut uulgus amicam,
sed pater ut gnatos diligit et generos.
nunc te cognoui: quare etsi impensius uror,
multo mi tamen es uilior et leuior.
qui potis est, inquis? quod amantem inuria talis
cogit amare magis, sed bene uelle minus.

72

Time was you said only Catullus could touch you,
that God in heaven couldn't have you before me.
I loved you then, not just as a guy does a girl,
but the way a father loves his sons and grandsons.
Now I know you, Lesbia, and if my passion grows,
you're also much cheaper to me and insignificant.
How's that? Because, hurt a man in love and he
lusts for you more, but the less he really cares.

LXXIII

Desine de quoquam quicquam bene uelle mereri
aut aliquem fieri posse putare pium.
omnia sunt ingrata, nihil fecisse benigne
prodest, immo etiam taedet obestque magis,
ut mihi, quem nemo grauius nec acerbius urget,
quam modo qui me unum atque unicum amicum habuit.

73

Get off it, people don't owe you any favors,
there's nobody who even knows what it means.
You get no thanks, doesn't pay to be decent,
it wears you out and they step all over you,
like me: nobody's ever fucked me up so bad
as someone who said I was his closest friend.

LXXIV

Gellius audierat patruum obiurgare solere,
siquis delicias diceret aut faceret.
hoc ne ipsi accideret, patrui perdepsuit ipsam
uxorem et patruum reddidit Harpocratem.
quod uoluit fecit: nam, quamuis irrumet ipsum
nunc patruum, uerbum non faciet patruus.

74

Gellius knew uncle would scream and holler
if one committed obscenity in word or in deed.
To get out of this, he did a job on his aunt
that struck uncle dumb as an Egyptian statue.
It worked out just fine. He can even bang
his uncle now: the old boy won't say a word.

LXXV

Huc est mens deducta tua, mea Lesbia, culpa,
atque ita se officio perdidit ipsa suo,
ut iam nec bene uelle queat tibi, si optima fias,
nec desistere amare, omnia si facias.

75

My mind's sunk so low, Lesbia, because of you,
wrecked itself on your account so bad already,
I couldn't like you if you were the best of women,
or stop loving you, no matter what you do.

LXXVI

Siqua recordanti benefacta priora uoluptas
est homini, cum se cogitat esse pium,
nec sanctam uiolasse fidem, nec foedere nullo
diuum ad fallendos numine abusum homines,
multa parata manent in longa aetate, Catulle,
ex hoc ingrato gaudia amore tibi.
nam quaecumque homines bene cuiquam aut dicere possunt
aut facere, haec a te dictaque factaque sunt.
omnia quae ingratae perierunt credita menti.
quare cur te iam amplius excrucies?
quin tu animo offirmas atque istinc teque reducis,
et dis inuitis desinis esse miser?
difficile est longum subito deponere amorem?
difficile est, uerum hoc qualubet efficias.
una salus haec est, hoc est tibi peruincendum,
hoc facias, siue id non pote siue pote.
o di, si uestrum est misereri, aut si quibus umquam
extremam iam ipsa in morte tulistis opem,
me miserum aspicite et, si uitam puriter egi,
eripite hanc pestem perniciemque mihi,
quae mihi subrepens imos ut torpor in artus
expulit ex omni pectore laetitias.
non iam illud quaero, contra me ut diligat illa,
aut, quod non potis est, esse pudica uelit:
ipse ualere opto et taetrum hunc deponere morbum.
o di, reddite mi hoc pro pietate mea.

76

If a man can take any pleasure remembering
good things he's done, knowing he's been true,
that he didn't break his word, or swear by the
gods to promises that he never meant to keep,
then many joys await you for long years to come,
Catullus, from this thankless love of yours.
Because all the things a person could ever say
or do for another, were said and done by you.
All wasted, given to a heart that never cared.
So why keep on torturing yourself anymore?
Come on now, be tough, get yourself together,
the gods don't want your misery, so quit it.
It's hard suddenly after so long to forget her?
Sure it's hard, but you've got to do it somehow.
It's the only way out, you must see it through.
Do it. Never mind if you can or you can't.
O gods! If you feel pity, if you ever gave
a man aid and comfort in death's last agony,
see my misery, and if I've lived a pure life,
tear out this wasting disease from inside me,
this slow paralysis that creeps through my body,
driving all the joy of life out of my heart!
I'm not asking that she love me back any longer,
or, the impossible, that she ever know shame;
I want myself well, to be rid of this sickness.
Do this for me, O gods, in reward for my piety.

LXXVII

Rufe mihi frustra ac nequiquam credite amice
(frustra? immo magno cum pretio atque malo),
sicine subrepsti mi, atque intestina perurens
ei misero eripuisti omnia nostra bona?
eripuisti, heu heu nostrae crudele uenenum
uitae, heu heu nostrae pestis amicitiae.

77

Rufus, I trusted you as a friend, for nothing.
Nothing? No, I paid, and it cost me plenty.
You sucked up to me, wormed your way inside,
and then you burnt me, you tore my guts out,
ripped them out, you're poison, you killed me,
what did you do, we were friends, you remember?

LXXVIII

Gallus habet fratres, quorum est lepidissima coniunx
alterius, lepidus filius alterius.
Gallus homo est bellus: nam dulces iungit amores,
cum puero ut bello bella puella cubet.
Gallus homo est stultus, nec se uidet esse maritum,
qui patruus patrui monstret adulterium.

78

Gallus has two brothers, one of whom has
a darling wife, and the other a darling son.
Gallus is a good man, he helps sweet love along
and brings the nice boy to the nice girl's bed.
Gallus is also stupid. He has a wife himself
and teaches his nephew to screw his own aunts.

LXXVIIIa

sed nunc id doleo, quod purae pura puella . . .
suauia comminxit spurca saliua tua.
uerum id non impune feres: nam te omnia saecla
noscent et, qui sis, fama loquetur anus.

78a

It bothers me that a sweet girl's sweet lips
got smeared all over with your slimy drool.
But you'll pay: people will get wise to what
you are, and pass the word on down through the ages.

LXXIX

Lesbius est pulcer. quid ni? quem Lesbia malit
quam te cum tota gente, Catulle, tua.
sed tamen hic pulcer uendat cum gente Catullum,
si tria notorum suauia reppererit.

79

Lesbius is one of the pretty boys, no wonder Lesbia
takes him over you and your whole family, Catullus.
Meanwhile pretty boy would sell off Catullus and family
for a couple of people who'd just say hello to him.

LXXX

Quid dicam, Gelli, quare rosea ista labella
hiberna fiant candidiore niue,
mane domo cum exis et cum te octaua quiete
e molli longo suscitat hora die?
nescio quid certe est: an uere fama susurrat
grandia te medii tenta uorare uiri?
sic certe est: clamant Victoris rupta miselli
ilia, et emulso labra notata sero.

80

Tell me why, Gellius, those rosy red lips
are so pale and white as the winter snow
whenever you wake up early in the morning
or after your nap in the long afternoon?
What can it be? Is it true what they say?
Do you eat a big thing men have up front?
Must be, look at poor Victor, both balls
busted, and your mouth all caked with goo.

LXXXI

Nemone in tanto potuit populo esse, Iuuenti,
bellus homo, quem tu diligere inciperes
praeterquam iste tuus moribunda ab sede Pisauri
hospes inaurata pallidior statua,
qui tibi nunc cordi est, quem tu praeponere nobis
audes, et nescis quod facinus facias?

81

Out of all these people, Juventius, isn't there
one decent man you could begin to appreciate
besides that stranger in from sick city Pisaurum
with a pasty face worse than a painted statue
and so dear to you now you dare to pick him over
me, and you don't even know what you're doing?

PISAURENSIS

LXXXII

Quinti, si tibi uis oculos debere Catullum
aut aliud si quid carius est oculis,
eripere ei noli, multo quod carius illi
est oculis seu quid carius est oculis.

82

Quintius, if you want me to owe you my life
or whatever more than my life I might care for,
don't tear me away from what I care for even
more than my life, yes, even more than my life.

LXXXIII

Lesbia mi praesente uiro mala plurima dicit:
haec illi fatuo maxima laetitia est.
mule, nihil sentis: si nostri oblita taceret,
sana esset: nunc quod gannit et obloquitur,
non solum meminit, sed, quae multo acrior est res,
irata est: hoc est, uritur et loquitur.

83

Lesbia curses me out in front of her husband
and the happy fool goes delirious.
Wise up, stupid. If she got over me she'd shut up
and act normal. So her bitching and snapping means
she remembers, and she's even nastier about it
because she's burnt. When in heat she hollers.

LESBIA

LXXXIV

'Chommoda' dicebat, si quando commoda uellet
dicere, et insidias Arrius 'hinsidias,'
et tum mirifice sperabat se esse locutum,
cum quantum poterat dixerat 'hinsidias.'
credo, sic mater, sic Liber auunculus eius,
sic maternus auus dixerat atque auia.
hoc misso in Syriam requierant omnibus aures:
audibant eadem haec leniter et leuiter,
nec sibi postilla metuebant talia uerba,
cum subito affertur nuntius horribilis:
Ionios fluctus, postquam illuc Arrius isset,
iam non Ionios esse, sed 'Hionios.'

84

When Arrius spoke on national economy, it was
'the heconomy,' internal subversion, 'hinternal,'
and he thought he sounded terrific, especially
harping on 'hinternal subversion' all the time.
Anyway, that's what his mother told him, and his
uncle, his grandmother, and his grandfather also.
Then he got sent to Syria, our ears had a rest,
we heard the same old words, but soft and easy,
and we worried no more about verbal disasters.
Then, all of a sudden, came the horrible news—
seems ever since Arrius landed in Asia, the place
isn't the same anymore—it's gone 'Hasiatic'!

LXXXV

Odi et amo. quare id faciam, fortasse requiris.
nescio, sed fieri sentio et excrucior.

85

I hate her and I love her. Don't ask me why.
It's the way I feel, that's all, and it hurts.

LXXXVI

Quintia formosa est multis. mihi candida, longa,
recta est: haec ego sic singula confiteor.
totum illud formosa nego: nam nulla uenustas,
nulla in tam magno est corpore mica salis.
Lesbia formosa est, quae cum pulcerrima tota est,
tum omnibus una omnis surripuit Veneres.

86

To most people Quintia's beautiful. Now she's
a handsome woman, tall, poised, I admit that,
but beautiful, no. There's no Venus in her,
not one ounce of bounce in her whole big body.
Lesbia's beautiful. She looks good all over,
and makes every Venus her personal property.

LXXXVII

Nulla potest mulier tantum se dicere amatam
uere, quantum a me Lesbia amata mea es.
nulla fides ullo fuit umquam in foedere tanta,
quanta in amore tuo ex parte reperta mea est.

87

No woman can ever say she was loved
as much as I loved you, my Lesbia.
And no vows were ever kept as well
as my love for you kept me to mine.

LXXXVIII

Quid facit is, Gelli, qui cum matre atque sorore
prurit et abiectis peruigilat tunicis?
quid facit is, patruum qui non sinit esse maritum?
ecquid scis quantum suscipiat sceleris?
suscipit, o Gelli, quantum non ultima Tethys
nec genitor Nympharum abluit Oceanus:
nam nihil est quicquam sceleris, quo prodeat ultra,
non si demisso se ipse uoret capite.

88

Tell me, Gellius, what's a man doing if he's up
all night naked screwing his mother and his sister?
Or edges out his uncle playing hubby to his aunt?
You know how much dirt the man gets on himself?
I'll tell you, Gellius: old man Ocean and his wife
and all their nymph daughters couldn't clean him up.
He's so far gone filthy there's no place to go,
even if he bends over and fucks himself in the face.

LXXXIX

Gellius est tenuis: quid ni? cui tam bona mater
tamque ualens uiuat tamque uenusta soror
tamque bonus patruus tamque omnia plena puellis
cognatis, quare is desinat esse macer?
qui ut nihil attingat, nisi quod fas tangere non est,
quantumuis quare sit macer inuenies.

89

Gellius looks skinny lately. Sure, what with
mother dear so ready and willing, sister so sweet,
and good old uncle and all those nieces around,
how in the hell could he help but be skinny?
With all he ought to be keeping his hands off,
there's enough to wear him right down to the bone.

GELLIUS

XC

Nascatur magus ex Gelli matrisque nefando
coniugio et discat Persicum aruspicium
(nam magus ex matre et gnato gignatur oportet,
si uera est Persarum impia religio)
gnatus ut accepto ueneretur carmine diuos,
omentum in flamma pingue liquefaciens.

90

Let Gellius and his mother keep on mating,
and may they produce a real wizard of a kid
(that's how you breed a Persian magician
from what I hear about the filthy religion)
so their son can send up hymns of praise
and burn guts in the fire to please the gods.

XCI

Non ideo, Gelli, sperabam te mihi fidum
in misero hoc nostro, hoc perdito amore fore,
quod te cognossem bene constantemue putarem
aut posse a turpi mentem inhibere probro,
sed neque quod matrem nec germanam esse uidebam
hanc tibi, cuius me magnus edebat amor.
et quamuis tecum multo coniungerer usu,
non satis id causae credideram esse tibi.
tu satis id duxti: tantum tibi gaudium in omni
culpa est, in quacumque est aliquid sceleris.

91

No, Gellius, I was hoping you'd be true to me
in this sorry mess, this doomed love of mine,
not because I knew you well, or trusted you,
or thought you could control your filthy mind,
but because I figured at least the girl I loved
wasn't your mother, or even a sister of yours.
True, we were pretty close ourselves, yet I
never believed that was reason enough for you.
But I guess it was. You get a thrill out of
anything, a little dirt is all that you need.

XCII

Lesbia mi dicit semper male nec tacet umquam
de me: Lesbia me dispeream nisi amat.
quo signo? quia sunt totidem mea: deprecor illam
assidue, uerum dispeream nisi amo.

92

Lesbia always talks bad about me, she never
shuts up about it. I swear she loves me.
How come? It's the same with me. I curse her
with a vengeance, and I swear I love her.

XCIII

Nil nimium studeo, Caesar, tibi uelle placere,
nec scire utrum sis albus an ater homo.

93

I've no big wish to please you, Caesar,
or to know who or what the hell you are.

XCIV

Mentula moechatur. moechatur mentula? certe.
hoc est quod dicunt, ipsa olera olla legit.

94

Prickface fucks. Really?
Sure. He's a fucking prick.

XCVI

Si quicquam mutis gratum acceptumue sepulcris
accidere a nostro, Calue, dolore potest,
quo desiderio ueteres renouamus amores
atque olim missas flemus amicitias,
certe non tanto mors immatura dolori est
Quintiliae, quantum gaudet amore tuo.

96

If a silent grave can take any comfort,
any solace at all, Calvus, from the pain
by which we live old loves again and cry
for the love of friends we turned away,
then Quintilia, I know, feels less pain
for her early death, than joy in your love.

XCVII

Non ita me di ament quicquam referre putaui,
utrumne os an culum olfacerem Aemilio.
nilo mundius hoc, nihiloque immundius illud,
uerum etiam culus mundior et melior:
nam sine dentibus est. os dentis sesquipedalis,
gingiuas uero ploxeni habet ueteris,
praeterea rictum qualem diffissus in aestu
meientis mulae cunnus habere solet.
hic futuit multas et se facit esse uenustum,
et non pistrino traditur atque asino?
quem siqua attingit, non illam posse putemus
aegroti culum lingere carnificis?

97

You wouldn't think it made much difference
sniffing around Aemilius' mouth or his asshole,
one being no better or worse than the other,
but I figure his ass is a whole lot better,
it's got no teeth. His mouth has teeth in it
a half a yard long, the gums are all rotten,
sagging down loose as an old covered wagon,
and when he smiles the lips spread open wide
like a mule's cunt dripping on a hot summer day.
This is the big lover the ladies all fuck for?
I'd plug his face with a horse dick instead.
A girl who'd go near a creep like that, she
could get down and ream a sick hangman's ass.

XCVIII

In te, si in quemquam, dici pote, putide Victi,
id quod uerbosis dicitur et fatuis.
ista cum lingua, si usus ueniat tibi, possis
culos et crepidas lingere carpatinas.
si nos omino uis omnes perdere, Victi,
hiscas: omnino quod cupis efficies.

98

You're it if anybody when they say putrid, Victius,
always full of shit and running off at the mouth.
With that tongue of yours you could go into business
licking people's assholes and the crap off their shoes.
And if you feel like wiping us all out for good,
just open your mouth one more time and you'll do it.

XCIX

Surripui tibi, dum ludis, mellite Iuuenti,
suauiolum dulci dulcius ambrosia.
uerum id non impune tuli: namque amplius horam
suffixum in summa me memini esse cruce,
dum tibi me purgo nec possum fletibus ullis
tantillum uestrae demere saeuitiae.
nam simul id factum est, multis diluta labella
guttis abstersisti omnibus articulis,
ne quicquam nostro contractum ex ore maneret,
tamquam commictae spurca saliua lupae.
praeterea infestum misero me tradere amori
non cessasti omnique excruciare modo,
ut mi ex ambrosia mutatum iam foret illud
suauiolum tristi tristius elleboro.
quam quoniam poenam misero proponis amori,
numquam iam posthac basia surripiam.

99

You were playing, Juventius, when I stole a kiss
that tasted sweeter to me than sweet ambrosia.
But I didn't get away with it. No, you had me
nailed to the cross, I remember, for hours after,
begging for forgiveness with tears in my eyes,
and you wouldn't budge, you were that mad at me.
Even the minute I did it you washed your lips
with water and wiped them off with your fingers,
so you wouldn't catch any disease from my mouth,
as if it were nasty spit from a sick old whore.
Then, because I wanted you so much, you made
me miserable, torturing me in all kinds of ways,
till that sweet little kiss went so bad finally,
it tasted bitter to me as bitterest hellebore.
If that's the way you punish a poor lover, okay,
from here on in I steal no more kisses from you.

CI

Multas per gentes et multa per aequora uectus
aduenio has miseras, frater, ad inferias,
ut te postremo donarem munere mortis
et mutam nequiquam alloquerer cinerem,
quandoquidem fortuna mihi tete abstulit ipsum,
heu miser indigne frater adempte mihi.
nunc tamen interea haec prisco quae more parentum
tradita sunt tristi munere ad inferias,
accipe fraterno multum manantia fletu,
atque in perpetuum, frater, aue atque uale.

101

I crossed many lands and a lot of ocean
to get to this painful ceremony, my brother,
so I could finally give you gifts for the dead,
and waste time talking to some silent ashes
being that you're not here yourself with me.
Fate did wrong, my brother, to tear us apart.
But I bring you these offerings now anyway,
after the old custom our parents taught us.
Take them, soaked with your brother's tears,
and forever more, my brother, goodbye.

CIII

Aut sodes mihi redde decem sestertia, Silo,
deinde esto quamuis saeuus et indomitus:
aut, si te nummi delectant, desine quaeso
leno esse atque idem saeuus et indomitus.

103

If you don't mind, give me my ten back, Silo,
and then go play tough guy all you like,
or if you love the money that much, do me a favor,
don't pimp and on top of that get tough with me.

CIV

Credis me potuisse meae maledicere uitae,
ambobus mihi quae carior est oculis?
non potui, nec, si possem, tam perdite amarem:
sed tu cum Tappone omnia monstra facis.

104

You think I could talk bad about her, my life,
dearer to me than these two eyes right here?
I couldn't. If I could I wouldn't love her so.
But you and Tappo make it all a big deal.

CV

Mentula conatur Pipleium scandere montem.
Musae furcillis praecipitem eiciunt.

105

Prickface tries to scale the heights of poetry.
With pitchforks the Muses poke him back down on his ass.

CVI

Cum puero bello praeconem qui uidet esse,
quid credat, nisi se uendere discupere?

106

If you spot a pretty boy out with an auctioneer,
what can you think but that he's looking to sell himself?

CVII

Si quicquam cupido optantique optigit umquam
insperanti, hoc est gratum animo proprie.
quare hoc est gratum, nobis quoque, carius auro,
quod te restituis, Lesbia, mi cupido.
restituis cupido atque insperanti, ipsa refers te
nobis. o lucem candidiore nota!
quis me uno uiuit felicior, aut magis hac res
optandas uita dicere quis poterit?

107

To get what one has always wanted but no longer
hoped for, that's what gives a heart life again.
So you gave me something more precious than gold,
Lesbia, when you came back to me. I wanted you,
kept on wanting you, and after I'd given up hope,
then you came back to me. What a day that was!
What man alive has ever been happier than I am?
Who could possibly want anything more out of life?

CVIII

Si, Comini, populi arbitrio tua cana senectus
spurcata impuris moribus intereat,
non equidem dubito quin primum inimica bonorum
lingua exsecta auido sit data uulturio,
effossos oculos uoret atro gutture coruus,
intestina canes, cetera membra lupi.

108

Cominius, if the people ever make up their mind
to finish you off for good in your dirty old age,
first your tongue, the enemy of all decent folks,
will be ripped out and fed to the hungry vultures,
your eyeballs gobbled down a black crow's gullet,
dogs'll get your guts, what's left, the wolves.

CIX

Iucundum, mea uita, mihi proponis amorem
hunc nostrum inter nos perpetuumque fore.
di magni, facite ut uere promittere possit,
atque id sincere dicat et ex animo,
ut liceat nobis tota perducere uita
aeternum hoc sanctae foedus amicitiae.

109

You promise me, my life, that this love of ours
will be happy, and will last forever between us.
Great gods, let her be able to keep this promise,
to say it in truth, from the bottom of her heart,
so that we may cherish for the rest of our lives
this eternal bond of sacred love and friendship.

CX

Aufilena, bonae semper laudantur amicae:
accipiunt pretium quae facere instituunt.
tu, quod promisti mihi quod mentita, inimica es:
quod nec das et fers, saepe facis facinus.
aut facere ingenuae est, aut non promisse pudicae,
Aufilena, fuit: sed data corripere
fraudando officiis, plus quam meretricis auarae,
quae sese toto corpore prostituit.

110

Everyone likes good, friendly women, Aufilena,
they get their price for what they deliver.
Now we had a deal and you didn't keep to it,
that isn't friendly. You take and don't give,
that's low. Either do the thing straight out
and true, or say no, the way a nice girl should,
but, Aufilena, to grab a man's money and then
hold out on the goods, that's greedier than a
cheap whore who hustles every hole in her body.

CXI

Aufilena, uiro contentam uiuere solo,
nuptarum laus ex laudibus eximiis:
sed cuiuis quamuis potius succumbere par est,
quam matrem fratres ex patruo . . .

111

Aufilena, to live content with just one husband
is for a married woman the highest praise of all.
But it's better to sleep around with everybody
than for a mother to bear brothers by their uncle.

CXII

Multus homo es, Naso, neque tecum multus homost qui
descendit: Naso, multus es et pathicus.

112

There's a lot of man in you
Naso, and a lot of men also.

CXIII

Consule Pompeio primum duo, Cinna, solebant
Maeciliam: facto consule nunc iterum
manserunt duo, sed creuerunt milia in unum
singula. fecundum semen adulterio.

113

In Pompey's first term as president, Cinna,
two made it with Maecilia. He's president again,
again there are two, but with three big O's
up there also. Love is a many-splendored thing.

CXIV

Firmano saltu non falso Mentula diues
fertur, qui tot res in se habet egregias,
aucupium omne genus, piscis, prata, aura ferasque.
nequiquam: fructus sumptibus exsuperat.
quare concedo sit diues, dum omnia desint.
saltum laudemus, dum modo ipse egeat.

114

It's no lie, Prickface is rich all right. He owns
real estate in Firmum, and it's got everything:
poultry, fish, dairy, produce, and wild game also.
Worthless, he spends it faster than he makes it.
So I say sure, he's rich, with plenty of nothing.
The property's high class, but the owner is broke.

CXV

Mentula habet instar triginta iugera prati,
quadraginta arui: cetera sunt maria.
cur non diuitiis Croesum superare potis sit,
uno qui in saltu tot bona possideat,
prata arua ingentes siluas altasque paludes
usque ad Hyperboreos et mare ad Oceanum?
omnia magna haec sunt, tamen ipsest maximus ultro,
non homo, sed uero Mentula magna minax.

115

Here's Prickface with over thirty acres of range,
forty of farmland, plus beach property besides.
Now anybody who can own plowed fields, pasture,
tracts of forest, and wetlands clear out to the
ocean's edge in one estate, the man's got to be
richer than Croesus himself, right? But, if you
think all this is great, he's still the greatest,
because he isn't even human like the rest of us
either, but a great big giant Prick on two legs.

CXVI

Saepe tibi studioso animo uenante requirens
carmina uti possem mittere Battiadae,
qui te lenirem nobis, neu conarere
tela infesta meum mittere in usque caput,
hunc uideo mihi nunc frustra sumptum esse laborem,
Gelli, nec nostras hic ualuisse preces.
contra nos tela ista tua euitabimus acta
at fixus nostris tu dabi' supplicium.

116

I thought and thought about how I could
send you some translations of Callimachus,
so you'd go easy on me, and stop trying
to throw all those damn spears at my head,
but I see now it's all been for nothing,
Gellius, even my prayers aren't worth it.
I'll just keep out of range, but you'll
beg for mercy when my spears start flying.

NOTES

Poem 1.   This dedicatory poem is addressed to Cornelius Nepos, historian and biographer. Like Catullus, he came from the province of Cisalpine Gaul. Catullus's "in a couple of pages" is not to be taken literally.

Poem 2.   Here is the first of some twenty-five poems Catullus wrote about his love affair with Lesbia. Doubts as to her identity persist, but the evidence points to Clodia, the most beautiful, abandoned, and dangerous woman we know of in her time.

Poem 6.   Flavius is one of many persons Catullus mentions by name who are otherwise unidentifiable. Most of them are omitted from these notes.

Poem 10.   Catullus was a member of the staff of C. Memmius, military governor of Bithynia, in 57-56 B.C. Varus is thought to be Alfenus Varus, a lawyer originally from Cisalpine Gaul who became consul in 39 B.C. He may be Alfenus in poem 30 as well.

Poem 11.   Furius is probably M. Furius Bibaculus, one of the circle of new poets of the day.

Poem 12.   Not much is known of Asinius Marrucinus, but his younger brother Pollio is almost certainly Asinius Pollio, orator and historian, and later a friend of Virgil and Horace.

Poem 14.   C. Licinius Calvus, an outspoken critic of Julius Caesar, was an orator and one of the new poets. He is remembered as Catullus's closest, most loyal friend. Vatinius, a political ally of Caesar mentioned by Catullus in other poems, was a favorite target of Calvus (see poem 53).

Poem 15.   Catullus's boyfriend is the Juventius of other poems.

Poem 26.   These are names for the South, West, North and East winds respectively.

Poem 28.   L. Calpurnius Piso Caesonius was Julius Caesar's father-in-law. He ruled as military governor of Macedonia in 57-55 B.C.

Poem 29.   Catullus addresses the first ten lines of this poem to Pompey, the next ten to Julius Caesar, and the last lines to both of them. Pompey was married to Caesar's daughter Julia, which made these two men of Rome's triumvirate in-laws. Mamurra, the main target of Catullus in this poem, was a Roman knight from Formiae who served under both Pompey in Pontus and Caesar in Spain and Gaul. He was notorious for having squandered vast sums of booty won in these conquests abroad. Catullus attacks him and Caesar together in poem 57. In other poems, Mamurra is singled out for abuse by Catullus under the epithet Mentula, or "Prickface." The term is slang in Latin for the penis.

Poem 35.   Caecilius's "Lady of Dindymus" refers to the goddess Cybele, the Great Mother. Priests in her worship castrated themselves. Catullus writes about this cult in one of his long poems, 63.

Poem 36.   ". . . old slow foot" is Vulcan, the god of fire, who was lame. Venus had temples to her worship in some places mentioned in this poem.

Poem 37.   "Brothers of the Beanie" refers to statues of the twins Castor and Pollux, depicted wearing caps signifying the elevation of slaves to the status of freedmen. The house is probably Clodia's residence.

Poem 38.   This might be Quintius Cornificius, an orator and one of the new poets. Simonides, mentioned in the original, was a Greek lyric poet (556-467 B.C.).

Poem 41.   Ameana is Mamurra's mistress.

Poem 44.   The Tiburtine district was fashionable, the Sabine was not. Publius Sestius was a well-known political figure with a reputation for making bad speeches.

Poem 49.   Marcus Tullius Cicero is the famous lawyer, orator, and statesman. Cicero, of an older generation, was disparaging of the new poets. He and Catullus had a good many friends and enemies in common, but their own relationship must have been strained.

Poem 51.   The first three stanzas are a partial translation by Catullus of a poem by Sappho, the seventh-century Greek poet of Lesbos. Poem 11 is written in the same meter, named the Sapphic strophe after her. They are the earliest known examples of Latin poetry in this form.

Poem 54a.   This is addressed to Julius Caesar.

Poem 56.   Cato here may be P. Valerius Cato, a poet and critic from Verona who is thought to have been the original source of the new movement in poetry.

Poem 58.   M. Caelius Rufus, orator and politician, is probably the Rufus of poems 69 and 77. He was one of Clodia's lovers. Cicero defended him against Clodia's charges of attempted poisoning in his *Pro Caelio* speech, and accused her in turn of incest with her brother, P. Clodius Pulcher. Catullus accuses her of the same in poem 79.

Poem 65.   Q. Hortensius Hortalus was an orator, a friend of Cicero, and a poet. Of Catullus's brother almost nothing more is known. The Greek poet Callimachus (died 250 B.C.) was much admired by the new poets. Poem 66, one of Catullus's long works, is no doubt the translation of Callimachus that Catullus refers to here.

Poem 68.   This letter in verse is followed by a long poem. The two are sometimes taken to be one poem, but they may be read separately.

Poem 74.   The "Egyptian statue" is that of the god Harpocrates (Horus), who was depicted with his finger stuck in his mouth.

Poem 79.   P. Clodius Pulcher, Clodia's brother, made a career for himself as a thug in Julius Caesar's pay. He led roving gangs who warred in the streets with those of rival factions, and lost his life in one such encounter. Catullus puns with the name Pulcher, which means "pretty."

Poem 83.   Clodia's husband was Q. Caecilius Metellus Celer, governor of Cisalpine Gaul in 62-61 B.C., and consul in 60 B.C. Clodia was suspected of having poisoned him.

Poem 84.   Arrius' "h's" are not a speech defect, but an overly zealous use of the Greek aspirate for rhetorical effect.

Poem 113.   C. Helvius Cinna was one of the new poets and a companion of Catullus on the staff of Memmius in Bithynia. He was mistaken for Cornelius Cinna, a conspirator against Julius Caesar, and murdered by a mob during Caesar's funeral.

AFTERWORD

Gaius Valerius Catullus was born in Verona in or about the year 84 B.C. His father was a prominant man in that city, of sufficient wealth and influence to entertain Julius Caesar in his home when Caesar was governor of Gaul. Even today, one may come across inscriptions bearing the family name Valerius in Verona.

Before he was twenty years old, Catullus came to Rome. Here he made the acquaintance, not always friendly, of some of the leading figures of the day in poetry and politics. Some of them are well known to us: Julius Caesar, Pompey, Cicero, Cornelius Nepos the biographer and historian, and the poet and orator Licinius Calvus, whose name was linked with Catullus's in later generations as a symbol of enduring friendship. Others, too, have left a trace in history: Memmius, who brought Catullus along on his staff when he was governor of the Black Sea province of Bithynia, or Caesar's lieutenant Mamurra, whom Catullus addressed also by a less complimentary name. Most of Catullus's circle, however, we learn of from his poems, and can be identified only dubiously or not at all with known historical persons: his friend Fabullus, for example, whom he invited once to dinner for a special treat, Furius and Aurelius, the unsavory Gellius, smiling Egnatius, flabby Thallus, delicious Ipsithilla, and the rest. It is an unforgettable crowd, a little short on manners, some of them, but more than making up for it in verve. One cannot help wanting to know more about these individuals, but the poems do not lose anything for that. They create for us vivid characters, people of every sort, all in all as full and fine a collection of types as we could hope to know.

Two times a special ardor burned in Catullus. One of these

loves was a boy named Juventius, for whom Catullus wrote several passionate poems. Catullus has always been remembered best, however, for his poems to the woman he called Lesbia. These poems, some twenty or thirty in all, seem to extend over the whole range of feeling, to tell a story of youthful infatuation, trials of infidelity, and, finally, the morbid anguish of hopeless and unquenchable desire. Many scholars have tried to make an orderly narrative out of these poems. There is evidence to suggest that Lesbia was a notorious woman named Clodia, wife of a onetime consul called Quintus Caecilius Metellus Celer and sister of one Publius Clodius Pulcher, a political thug in the service of Caesar. Cicero has left us a portrait of this lady in a wicked speech, full of innuendoes about depravity, even incest, which he delivered in defense of her former lover, Marcus Caelius Rufus. (Catullus addresses a Caelius and also a Rufus in some of his poems, and the object of them might well be Cicero's man.) However this might be, all we know of Catullus's passion is what he tells us in his poems. Each reader will fashion for himself an image of that love, and it will be his own. That is part of the fascination of the Lesbia poems, and an interpreter would be ungenerous to insist upon his own vision of it.

The kind of poetry which Catullus and his friends wrote was not conventional. Cicero refers, rather disparagingly, to some "nouveaux" poets (he uses a Greek word, *neoteroi*), moderns, we might say, and Catullus was the most famous of this group. Others in the circle were Catullus's own Calvus, Cornificius, of whom Catullus begs some consolatory verse, his friends Caecilius and Helvius Cinna, and one Furius Bibaculus, who may well be the Furius of Catullus's poems. The unfortunate Gellius may also have been a member of this coterie. Some of Catullus's poems are about poetry, and he is a frank and passionate critic. Making poems, for him, had the intensity of love itself.

The innovations of the group were various. Catullus experimented with meters that had not been tried in Latin before. He made use of colloquial language, or old-fashioned language, or words of his own invention, whenever it suited him. He brought poetry to everyday life, and in so doing extended its range of subjects and feelings. This is not to say, of course, that his poems were necessarily casual. For another mark of that circle of moderns was their interest in difficult forms and styles which Greek poets had developed, and they carefully worked allusions to this tradition into their verses. Even the simplest, most direct poems of Catullus can often be shown to depend upon a sophisticated handling of well-worn themes and figures. In fact, the standard epithet for Catullus among later Romans was *doctus*, which means "learned." Yet the poems wear their learning so lightly we scarcely notice it. If we catch an echo now and again of some familiar idea or phrase, it is fairly sure to be so fresh and fitting that we overlook Catullus's erudition, which made it possible, and wonder at the feel, the light and perfect touch which graces his poems. That is why some prefer to think that *doctus* refers to poetic skill, or to taste, in a word, to the sheer genius of the man.

To describe the quality of Catullus's poetry is not easy. Whole volumes have been given to the task. But if a word must suffice, I should say that his poems are alive. They all speak directly to someone, and they report what Catullus feels. Every feeling is there: gratitude, resentment, love, hate, something made up of love and hate which has no name but Catullus feels it and utters it all the same, the joy of Lesbia returning, grief at the death of his brother, spite, jealousy, rage, irony, contempt and amusement, everything—the range is so wide that it is a pleasure to make a list of them. And of every mood he knows the style. No one will doubt that Catullus is a master of the fine art of insult. Add to that his expert ability to tell a good joke with a keen eye for the ridiculous and a perfect sense of timing that still sets readers laughing at Egnatius, or Gellius, or Aemilius, or at Catullus himself. Or if he turns a tender verse or ventures a more exalted mode, it is with equal grace. Alive with passion, graceful and direct—these are the chief qualities of his poems.

Catullus, then, was rich in wit, in feeling, in art. He was also a serious man, with an old-fashioned high-mindedness. He had high expectations of friends and lovers, wanted loyalty, trust, a lifelong soul-deep bond of faith. When he feels that he has been betrayed, his pain and rage are shattering. Beneath the scurrilous banter and unrestrained emotions is a stern morality. What he demands of Lesbia is virtue.

In a way, Catullus's poems represent the conflicting values of his times. All currents crossed in Rome in the first century B.C. The city commanded an empire on three continents, which Roman farmers had conquered in centuries of war. Those years had nursed a stony ethic: duty, reliability, obedience to superiors, above all to the near boundless authority of the elder of the clan. All honor lay in service to the republic; private passions were suspect. Marriages were contracted by fathers for their sons and daughters. Social interests governed such arrangements, and feelings were left to follow, when they would. Tradition, the ways of the ancestors, governed the customs and ideals of that age.

By Catullus's day, however, the wealth and power of Rome had changed the city's character. Men and women yielded to more personal desires. They were distracted by love, which older generations had regarded as an adolescent madness. Some withdrew from public life and sought the peace of philosophic contemplation. Others turned from the formal cults managed by the state, to worship mysterious gods from the east that promised ecstasy. Baser desires also flourished. Greed and ambition were unrestrained. Pure passion seemed to be vindicated.

Catullus lived with these extremes. His poems challenge the repressive virtues of the old republic, while at the same time they lay bare the fickle and selfish desires which his own age more and more indulged. There is a tragic side to Catullus, for he did not find a love at once spontaneous and true. Certainly he did not find it with Lesbia.

Catullus was hostile also to the demagogy of Rome's new politicians. All the while Rome was extending her dominions, wealth and slaves streamed back into Italy. Independent farmers, who had formerly been the mainstay of the republic, were now increasingly displaced from the land by great plantations and ranches manned by slave labor. Many migrated to the city, others found careers as soldiers. Generals like Caesar and Pompey, relying upon the personal loyalties of their armies and catering to the aspirations of the people with bribes and promises, struggled with each other for supremacy in the state.

Catullus lived in the middle of a century of civil wars, which finally brought about the failure of the republic and the establishment of the principate, the empire at Rome. He was disgusted at the naked self-interest, perversity and brutality of these new leaders, and his attacks on Julius Caesar left an eternal stain upon Caesar's reputation, according to the ancient biographer Suetonius. We are told also that Catullus's father used his influence to patch over the feud between his son and Caesar. We may doubt, however, that Catullus was ever reconciled to the schemes and ambitions of Caesar and his son-in-law and rival, Pompey the Great. But neither did he preserve any faith in the haughty conservatives who cloaked their indecision or corruption in a mantle of antique virtue. In politics, as in love, Catullus seems to have faced harsh realities with open eyes. His poems, therefore, are more than personal; they give expression also to the crisis of his age.

So directly and easily does Catullus speak to our time, that it is difficult sometimes to believe that his world is two millennia removed from ours. It is indeed a lucky accident that we have his poems at all. In antiquity, he was most highly regarded. He exerted a powerful influence upon Virgil, who acknowledged his debt many times by imitating or adapting some fine phrase or sentiment of Catullus's. Propertius remarked that Catullus had made Lesbia more famous than Helen of Troy. Ovid revered him, as did Martial. Pliny, who was also from northern Italy, was proud to call him his own. The novelist Apuleius knew his poems—it is Apuleius who tells us that Lesbia is really Clodia—and other learned men of the later empire comment upon his verse.

But the Middle Ages were not kind to Catullus. Only a single manuscript of the collection, preserved at the cathedral library in Verona, is known to have survived the decline of classical culture, and it is only through copies of this text, rediscovered in the fourteenth century, that we enjoy the lyric poems of Catullus.

Carl Sesar's versions have brought Catullus to life. Catullus, too, was a translator, and to recreate the poetry of a master is a poet's work. Catullus speaks here in his own voice, full of wit and passion. The poems here are true translations, faithful in spirit and in detail to the original. The reader who finds delight in these poems, a hearty laugh or a sigh, is responding still, over the centuries and through the medium of a gifted translation, to the genius of Catullus.

David Konstan
Associate Professor of Classics
Wesleyan University

NOTE ON FURTHER READING

There are a great many studies of Catullus. Those who would like to pursue more fully some of the subjects discussed above, or who might enjoy a closer acquaintance with the Latin text, will find the following works helpful and conveniently available. Kenneth Quinn, *Catullus: The Poems* (Macmillan: London, 1970) provides very fine notes on points of syntax and interpretation, and useful references to special studies of individual poems. C. J. Fordyce, *Catullus* (Oxford: London, 1961) offers extensive commentary on an expurgated selection of the poems, and Elmer T. Merrill, *Catullus* (Harvard: Cambridge, Mass., 1951; originally 1893) is a sound and sensible commentary somewhat in the Victorian spirit. Among the volumes of general criticism in English are E. A. Havelock, *The Lyric Genius of Catullus* (Blackwell: Oxford, 1939), Kenneth Quinn, *Catullus: An Interpretation* (Batsford: London, 1972), and A. L. Wheeler, *Catullus and the Traditions of Ancient Poetry* (University of California: San Francisco, 1934).